Great Expectations

Charles Dickens

Guide written and developed by
John Mahoney and Stewart Martin

Charles Letts & Co Ltd
London, Edinburgh & New York

First published 1987
by Charles Letts & Co Ltd
Diary House, Borough Road, London SE1 1DW

Illustration: Peter McClure

Stewart Martin is an Honours graduate of Lancaster University, where he read English
and Sociology. He has worked both in the UK and abroad as a writer, a teacher, and an
educational consultant. He is married with three children, and is currently deputy
headmaster at Ossett School in West Yorkshire.

John Mahoney has taught English for twenty years. He has been head of English
department in three schools and has wide experience of preparing students at all levels
for most examination boards. He has worked both in the UK and North America
producing educational books and computer software on English language and literature.
He is married with three children and lives in Worcestershire.

British Library Cataloguing in Publication Data
  Mahoney, John
  Great expectations: Charles Dickens: guide.
  (Guides to literature)
  1. Dickens, Charles, 1812–1870, Great expectations
  I. Title   II. Martin, Stewart
  III. Dickens, Charles, 1812–1870, Great expectations
  IV. Series
  823'.8   PR4560

ISBN 0 85097 771 1

Printed and bound in Great Britain by
Charles Letts (Scotland) Ltd

Contents

To the student

This study companion to your English literature text acts as a guide to the novel or play being studied. It suggests ways in which you can explore content and context, and focuses your attention on those matters which will lead to an understanding, appreciative and sensitive response to the work of literature being studied.

Whilst covering all those aspects dealt with in the traditional-style study aid, more importantly, it is a flexible companion to study, enabling you to organize the patterns of study and priorities which reflect your particular needs at any given moment.

Whilst in many places descriptive, it is never prescriptive, always encouraging a sensitive personal response to a work of literature, rather than the shallow repetition of others' opinions. Such objectives have always been those of the good teacher, and have always assisted the student to gain high grades in 16+ examinations in English literature. These same factors are also relevant to students who are doing coursework in English literature for the purposes of continual assessment.

The major part of this guide is the 'Commentary' where you will find a detailed commentary and analysis of all the important things you should know and study for your examination. There is also a section giving practical help on how to study a set text, write the type of essay that will gain high marks, prepare coursework and a guide to sitting examinations.

Used sensibly, this guide will be invaluable in your studies and help ensure your success in the course.

Charles Dickens

Charles Dickens was born on 7 February 1812, in Portsmouth, the second of eight children. His father, John, was a clerk in the Naval Pay Office and was a jolly man, but irresponsible with money, which caused the family a great deal of hardship.

In 1817 Charles moved to Chatham, where his father had a job in the dockyard. This area of Kent – Rochester and the surrounding countryside – was loved by Charles, and many of his books are based there. He enjoyed his schooling in Rochester and used the opportunity to read widely. A maid in the household, Mary Weller, told Charles many frightening stories which fuelled and enriched his imagination.

There were no schooling arrangements when the family moved to London in 1822, because his father was deeply in debt. They lived a poverty-stricken existence and eventually Charles's father was imprisoned in Marshalsea debtors' prison. His wife and children joined him, as was the custom, but Charles had to fend for himself and obtained, at the age of twelve, a terrible job in a blacking factory pasting labels onto bottles. His experience of the factory conditions, and the exploitation of cheap labour and children, affected him deeply, and we find his concern for the way society treated children in many of his novels.

When his father was eventually released, Charles was able to go to school for a few years, until the age of fifteen. He then worked in a solicitors' office in Gray's Inn, where he learnt shorthand and reported the events of law courts, eventually becoming a reporter for the *Morning Chronicle*. Many of his observations and characters which appeared in later books were based on his experience, gained during this period of law and Parliament.

He wrote a set of short stories and called them *Sketches by Boz*, which was the nickname of a favourite brother. He followed this with *Pickwick Papers*, a novel that was very popular. It was written in serial form and people queued to purchase editions.

In 1836 he married Catherine Hogarth; her young sister Mary also lived with them but died, much to Charles's grief, in 1837. Another sister, Georgina, was a great friend. Dickens quickly became famous, moved to imposing houses with servants and had a large family. However, he was not happily married.

He travelled extensively and went to America in 1842. He also edited *Household Words* in which *Hard Times* appeared in 1857 to revive the flagging subscription. It was at this time that he became enthralled by, and a keen supporter of, amateur dramatics. In 1856 he bought Gad's Hill Place, a house he had much admired, in Rochester. His marriage was breaking apart and it is thought that he had an affair with an actress, Ellen Ternan. He left his wife in 1858, amidst a great scandal.

He lived alone at Gad's Hill and was drawn into his new interest – dramatic readings of his works. With his one-man show, he travelled extensively around England and America. He was an excellent actor and, supported only by desk and book, played all the parts. It was very exhausting, but although very ill, he insisted on continuing. Eventually, though, he had to stop and he retired to Gad's Hill to write. On 8 June 1870 he had a stroke and died the following day at the age of only fifty-eight, tended by Georgina, his wife's sister. He was buried in Westminster Abbey.

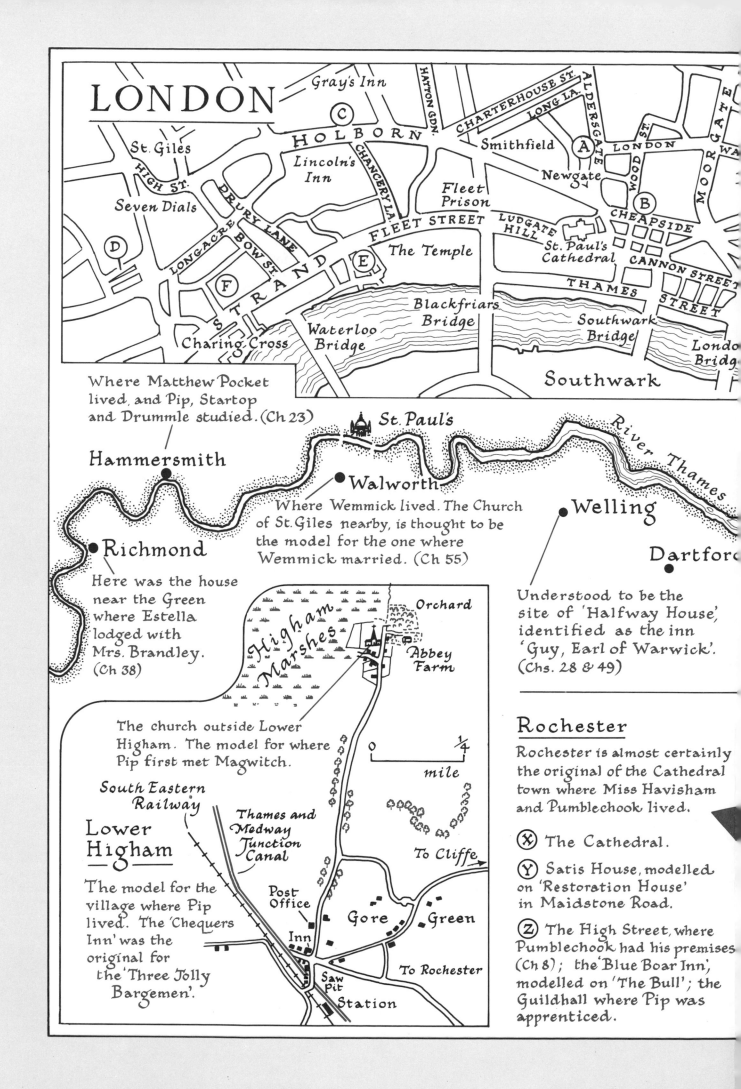

LONDON

Gray's Inn

CHARTERHOUSE ST.

LONG LA.

ALDERSGATE

St. Giles

HOLBORN

ⓒ

Lincoln's Inn

Smithfield

LONDON

WOOD ST.

Ⓐ

MOORGATE

HIGH ST.

Seven Dials

DRURY LANE

BOW ST.

LONGACRE

Fleet Prison

Newgate

Ⓑ

CHANCERY LA.

FLEET STREET

LUDGATE HILL

CHEAPSIDE

ⓓ

Ⓕ

Ⓔ

The Temple

St. Paul's Cathedral

CANNON STREET

STRAND

Blackfriars Bridge

THAMES STREET

Charing Cross

Waterloo Bridge

Southwark Bridge

London Bridge

Southwark

Where Matthew Pocket lived, and Pip, Startop and Drummle studied. (Ch 23)

St. Paul's

River Thames

Hammersmith

Walworth

Welling

Where Wemmick lived. The Church of St. Giles nearby, is thought to be the model for the one where Wemmick married. (Ch 55)

Dartford

Richmond

Here was the house near the Green where Estella lodged with Mrs. Brandley. (Ch 38)

Higham Marshes

Orchard

Abbey Farm

Understood to be the site of 'Halfway House', identified as the inn 'Guy, Earl of Warwick'. (Chs. 28 & 49)

The church outside Lower Higham. The model for where Pip first met Magwitch.

0   ¼
         mile

Rochester

Rochester is almost certainly the original of the Cathedral town where Miss Havisham and Pumblechook lived.

South Eastern Railway

Thames and Medway Junction Canal

To Cliffe

ⓧ The Cathedral.

Lower Higham

The model for the village where Pip lived. The 'Chequers Inn' was the original for the 'Three Jolly Bargemen'.

Post Office

Gore   Green

ⓨ Satis House, modelled on 'Restoration House' in Maidstone Road.

Inn

To Rochester

ⓩ The High Street, where Pumblechook had his premises (Ch 8); the 'Blue Boar Inn', modelled on 'The Bull'; the Guildhall where Pip was apprenticed.

Saw Pit

Station

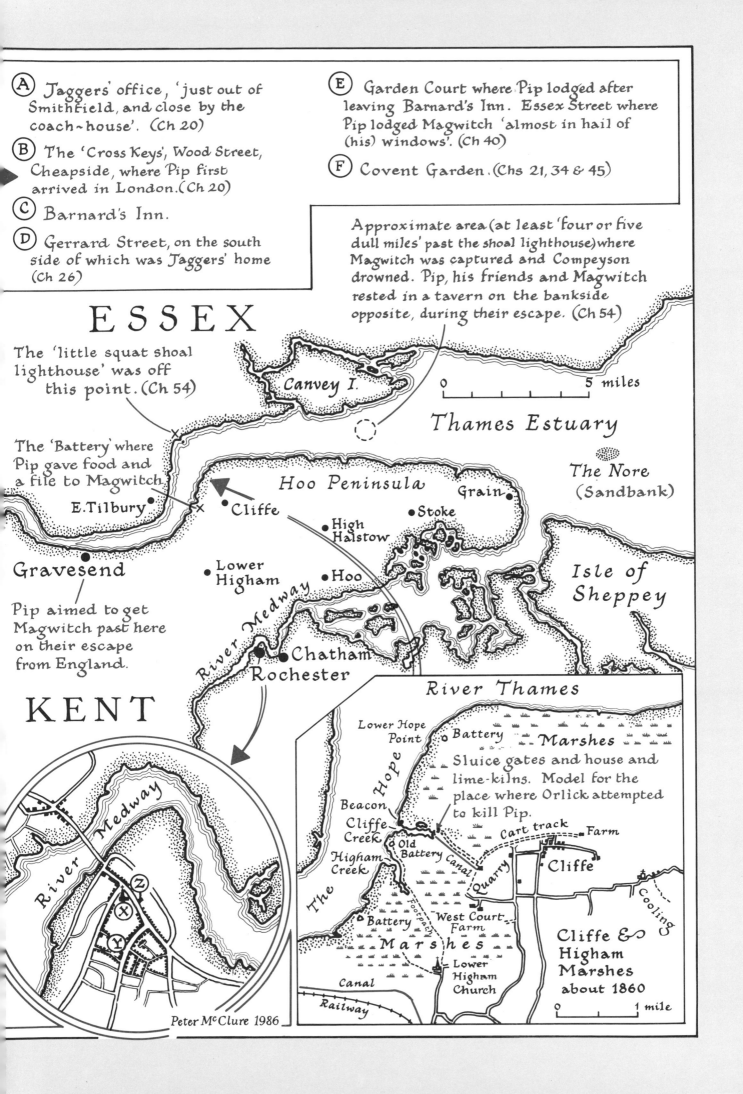

(A) Jaggers' office, 'just out of Smithfield, and close by the coach-house'. (Ch 20)

(B) The 'Cross Keys', Wood Street, Cheapside, where Pip first arrived in London. (Ch 20)

(C) Barnard's Inn.

(D) Gerrard Street, on the south side of which was Jaggers' home (Ch 26)

(E) Garden Court where Pip lodged after leaving Barnard's Inn. Essex Street where Pip lodged Magwitch 'almost in hail of (his) windows'. (Ch 40)

(F) Covent Garden. (Chs 21, 34 & 45)

Approximate area (at least 'four or five dull miles' past the shoal lighthouse) where Magwitch was captured and Compeyson drowned. Pip, his friends and Magwitch rested in a tavern on the bankside opposite, during their escape. (Ch 54)

ESSEX

The 'little squat shoal lighthouse' was off this point. (Ch 54)

Canvey I.

Thames Estuary

0   5 miles

The 'Battery' where Pip gave food and a file to Magwitch.

E. Tilbury

Hoo Peninsula

Grain

The Nore (Sandbank)

Gravesend

Pip aimed to get Magwitch past here on their escape from England.

Cliffe

High Halstow

Stoke

Lower Higham

Hoo

Isle of Sheppey

River Medway

KENT

Chatham
Rochester

River Thames

Lower Hope Point

Battery

Marshes

Sluice gates and house and lime-kilns. Model for the place where Orlick attempted to kill Pip.

Beacon

Cliffe Creek

Cart track

Farm

Old Battery

Canal

Quarry

Cliffe

Higham Creek

The

Footpath

West Court Farm

Cooling

Battery

Lower Higham Church

Cliffe & Higham Marshes about 1860

River Medway

Z

X

Y

Canal

Railway

0   1 mile

Peter McClure 1986

Understanding Great Expectations

An exploration of the major topics and themes in the novel

Summaries of themes

Expectations

It would be a mistake to see only Pip as having 'great expectations'; indeed, his expectations and desire to be a gentleman flow directly from the expectations of others, in particular Magwitch, who makes a fortune with the intention of using his money to turn Pip into a gentleman. Parallel to Magwitch's plans for the uplifting of Pip are those of Miss Havisham, whose desire is to take revenge on the breed of 'gentlemen' who so brutally destroyed her hopes and expectations. She plans to do this by turning Estella into a bewitching temptress of men whose beautiful exterior hides a hard interior which is contemptuous of men. Fortunately, neither Miss Havisham nor Magwitch succeed in turning their respective protégés into the exact image of the expectations they had in mind.

The great expectations of Pip and their implications are also amplified and reflected in the aspirations and expectations of numerous other characters. Herbert Pocket is an obvious point of comparison when we consider Pip's changing fortunes and his aspiration to become a gentleman. Bentley Drummle provides a nice counterpoint for Herbert and at the same time serves to frustrate Pip's love for Estella. The real gentleman of the novel, Joe Gargery, whose only desire is to do 'what's right' by those around him, provides a stark contrast for all the scheming and conniving of the other characters, so much so that he almost seems to be too much of a caricature. However, do keep in mind those qualities of the 'gentle Christian man' that he exemplifies; in doing so he provides a benchmark against which we can measure the attitudes and aspirations of other characters.

As you read the novel you should consider to what it is that characters like Pumblechook, Wopsle, Orlick and the Pockets aspire. Does Mrs Joe have any expectations; do Jaggers and Wemmick? What about the mass of people who frequent Little Britain and haunt Jaggers' office; what are their expectations?

Money A major aspect of many of the characters' aspirations has to do with the acquisition of wealth. Wemmick's concern to lay his hands on 'portable property' is perhaps the extreme example, but Pip's aspiration to become a gentleman is fuelled by his expectations of coming into great wealth. However, Pip's wealth and his joy in it turn to dust when he discovers its true source and he fails to follow Wemmick's injunction to acquire Magwitch's 'portable property': the notebook containing the details and deeds of his fortune. Ironically, in failing to acquire this easily won wealth, Pip sows the seeds which enable him to become a true gentleman – can you see how?

Be aware of the uses to which Pip puts his wealth in the middle stages of the novel. His extravagant style of living drives him away from Joe and into the arms of the debt collectors. The only really useful thing he does with it is to set Herbert on the road to a secure future, ironically also providing for himself, in the long term, the possibility of securing his own future. His inability to continue funding Herbert drives him to seek Miss Havisham's assistance, and thereby lays the foundation for her change of heart.

Joe's attitude to money is very clear. He willingly accepts the money due to him for the apprenticeship of Pip, but rejects the suggestion offered by Jaggers of making a profit by agreeing to release Pip so that Pip might pursue his expectations. He obviously feels that the money Pip is given by the mysterious benefactor acts as a barrier between them, largely because it changes Pip.

Do look out for the other characters' attitudes to money and wealth, the uses they are put to and the opportunities which a lack of money denies them.

Gentleman The acquisition of wealth is clearly associated in Pip's mind with the status of 'gentleman'. Within a short time he is elevated from the position of a blacksmith's boy to companion of a beautiful girl, and then to become a person of great expectations. The lure of money and a girl of education and 'breeding' lead to Pip adopting a lifestyle which takes no account of the true mark of a gentleman. His clothing, the acquisition of the Avenger, his feeling that Joe was not a suitable acquaintance for him in London, his anguish at Magwitch's manners, all highlight the false understanding he has of what makes a gentleman. What do other characters consider to be the mark of gentility?

The question 'What is a gentleman?' is central to the novel's concerns and therefore to Pip's expectations. Drummle was born to be a gentleman, but is not one – why? Herbert Pocket has both the temperament and breeding of a gentleman but has no money and little in the way of real prospects – does that make him less of a gentleman? The snobbery that various characters demonstrate in their dealings with each other is a particular feature of a mistaken view of gentility and one that Pip is very much guilty of in his attitude towards Joe. The gradual changes that occur in Pip's character enable us to follow his emerging awareness of what actually makes a gentleman and finally provides the answer to the question, 'Can Pip become a real gentleman?'

Guilt and   A particular feature of Pip's life are the feelings of guilt which pervade his early life and
redemption which affect his later relationship with Joe. They connect various strands of his life: guilt for the theft of food and a file for Magwitch; guilt for his lies about what happens at Satis House; guilt for his rejection of Joe in the middle stages of the novel. It is Magwitch who provides the money to turn him into a gentleman. It is Miss Havisham who falsely nurtures his desires to love Estella and become a gentleman. It is Joe who stands as a nagging reminder to Pip's conscience.

Redemption for Pip's actions comes about only when he has learned the true values of love, friendship and money, and the falseness of social aspirations, pretensions and snobbishness. He is, in fact, redeemed when he becomes a true gentleman. In that redemption he gives back to Magwitch all that Magwitch had ever hoped for, plus the news that his daughter is alive and loved by Pip. To Miss Havisham he gives forgiveness and great comfort at the end of a bitter life. To Joe he gives the joy of knowing that his Pip is a true gentleman at last.

Structure

The novel is structured in three clear parts, with nineteen chapters in the first part and twenty chapters in each of the next two. These three large sections of virtually equal length respectively cover Pip's boyhood, youth and maturity. A close examination of the aspects of suspense and mystery in the novel will help identify those divisions into thirty-six weekly instalments in which form the novel first appeared; they are not always identified by the editors of the various published editions.

Structural Notice how each of the subdivisions in the first section of the novel is reflected in the
pattern   third section where Pip's expectations find their fulfilment, though not in the ways he expected.

Stage 1: Pip's childhood in the marshes
Chapters 1– 6: Pip's first encounter with Magwitch
Chapters 7–11: Pip introduced to Miss Havisham and Estella
Chapters 12–17: Orlick's attack on Mrs Joe
Chapters 18–19: Pip's departure from the Old Forge

In the final paragraph of chapter 19 Pip comments 'We changed again, and yet again . . .'. Pip is about to embark on a new life which will indeed represent a change in all his old values and friendships.

Stage 2: Pip's youthful excesses in London and the loss of his moral values

Chapters 20–27: Pip learns how to conduct himself in presence of others, but forgets how to treat his old friend Joe

Chapters 28–35: Pip's infatuation for Estella grows. He continues to neglect Joe. He 'enjoys' 'The Finches of the Grove'

Chapters 36–39: With his generosity to Herbert, Drummle's relationship with Estella and return of Magwitch, Pip's life-style and attitudes suddenly begin a drastic change – for the better

In the final sentence of chapter 39, a new day dawns, the old candles are 'wasted out', the fire 'was dead'. Do these images represent the end of Pip's old ways and perhaps prompt us to expect the rebirth of a new Pip?

Stage 3: Pip's return to his birthplace; the abandoning of his false values and expectations; his maturing into manhood

Chapters 40–46: Second meeting between Pip and Magwitch

Chapters 47–51: Change in Miss Havisham's nature and Estella's true parentage revealed

Chapters 52–56: Orlick reappears and is apprehended. Magwitch's time runs out

Chapters 57–59: Pip's return to the forge, a very different person from the boy who left all those years ago. Pip and Estella meet again

The final paragraph, 'I took her hand in mine . . . I saw no shadow of another parting from her', fulfils the hope which was perhaps suggested in that last sentence of the second section of Pip's history.

Style and form

The novel is in the first person autobiographical form, that is, it is Pip who looks back on his past life and recounts the events which led to the situation we find him in at the last chapter. Chief characteristics of the style are the simplicity of the prose, the humour and the evocation of emotion. Dickens uses caricature to create some memorable people, and satire and irony on occasions to highlight his points. Realism is found in his settings, and in his recreation of the spoken language of the working and leisured classes, reflecting Dickens's firsthand knowledge of people, places and work.

For each of the points made in the previous paragraph you should be able to suggest events, places and characters which illustrate those aspects mentioned. For example, Joe is often thought of as being a caricature but as you read the commentary and the text you should actually see him as being a more rounded character than that. If he is but a caricature, how would you describe Pumblechook? There is certainly more to Joe than there is in the latter character. The novel's themes are serious and many of the settings are threatening and sordid. However, Dickens's use of humour provides welcome contrasts and diverts the reader with comic relief, creating vitality in the narrative. Humour can be found in the characterization (e.g. Aged Parent), the dialogue, the description and the action. Can you think of appropriate examples?

Charles Dickens uses the format of the traditional fairy tale as a vehicle through which to tell his story; you may perhaps recognize stories in which the poor little orphan sets out to make his fortune in the great city. But here the author has chosen to make the story one where the orphan does *not* make his fortune (though that is what the hero sets out to do). Instead, Dickens demonstrates the gradual evolution of the moral development of his hero in the face of the sudden acquisition and subsequent loss of fortune. The discovery of Pip's real benefactor and his associated loss of fortune coincides with an improvement in his moral and psychological growth.

There are other clear parallels with fairy stories, but again the author has changed the normal pattern of events. The evil and frightening old man turns out to be Pip's caring benefactor. The kindly old grandmother, Miss Havisham, turns out to be a vindictive old woman, and the 'beautiful princess' is shown to be a cold, almost inhuman figure. The ordinary perceptions of good and evil are, to an extent, obscured in Pip's search for the status of 'gentleman', and it is some time before he is able to make a clear judgment on the appearances of things and people and their reality.

Mystery and secrecy

Pip is surrounded by mystery and secrecy from the opening chapter to the novel's end. The two major figures who affect his life, Miss Havisham and Magwitch, are inextricably linked through Pip and Estella, though their exact relationships are not discovered until the reader is well into the story. Pip's mysterious benefactor and the strangers who approach him in the same public house, but on different occasions, the figure who follows him about London, the shadowy and threatening presence of Compeyson, all conspire to create a mood of suspense which permeates the whole story. It is a mood which finds ample reflection and support in the murky atmosphere of the marshes and the back streets of London. There are other secrets, and mysteries to be solved. Be aware of them!

Social aspects

This novel is not just the story of Pip and his expectations; it also contains a strong seam of social comment which is particularly relevant to the society of Dickens's time.

Criminals   Dickens is partly an observer and analyst of society and partly a moralist speaking about standards of right and wrong. In looking at his view of the criminal world you should be aware of the author's concerns. He never says Magwitch is a victim of society or that the prisons are filled with people who are there as a result of their desperate conditions in a harsh, class-divided world, yet the implications are present and the call for reform is presented in a way that could awake the public conscience. The scene where Pip goes before the magistrates to sign the apprenticeship papers is depressing enough, but it finds an even more frightening parallel view of the courts in the scene where Magwitch is sentenced.

Throughout the novel Dickens implies his personal condemnation of an inhuman legal system. He demonstrates this through Magwitch's story, Jaggers' cold professionalism, and scenes in Newgate and the trial. In *Great Expectations* the gentleman criminal, in the person of Compeyson, is seen to get a lighter sentence than Magwitch due to his appearance, yet in reality his is the greater crime. The ability to pay for a good defence is often more important than whether or not one is guilty or innocent, and Jaggers' skill at manipulating the law is one that not everyone can afford. Justice, in Dickens's time, very often depended more on the state of one's pocket and social standing than on the proof of one's guilt. One of the great ironies of the novel is that Pip's expectations are dependent upon a criminal's money.

Education   Education figures as a theme in this novel in two ways; there are passages which describe the formal process of learning, for Biddy and Pip, and others which reflect on the problems caused by a lack of learning – on the part of both Joe and Magwitch. Yet we better understand Pip as a product of both miseducation from Mrs Joe, Miss Havisham and Pumblechook, and of the lack of guidance which Pip needs to steer a successful course through his expectations.

Society   The social theme of the novel arises from the interaction of Pip with the other characters, ranging from the working man, Joe, to the leisured Finches and Miss Havisham. Pip's desire to become a gentleman is seen against the backdrop of the social position and pretensions of other characters. In this way the reader sees that the influences working on Pip are spread throughout the whole society. In observing Pip's movement from the position of a lowly blacksmith's boy, to that of the unproductive man of leisure and then to a hard-working businessman, we meet a whole range of people who reflect the society in which Dickens lived. Some of them are much larger than life, but their caricatures serve a very effective purpose.

Imagery

We are only considering here some of the major images which occur in this novel; others will be mentioned in the commentary. However, do read sensitively and look for those many other images which abound in the story and which support and clarify the author's writing and purposes.

Clothes   Clothing can act symbolically in representing the mental condition of the wearer: an obvious case in point is Miss Havisham. It can also create an illusion, particularly that one is a gentleman; note how Pip and Compeyson find their dress important to them, and how Magwitch reacts to and appears in the clothes found for him by Pip and Herbert.

Darkness

Images of darkness, shadows, mist and lack of light abound in *Great Expectations*. The darkness surrounding Pip is seen in the landscape, the city, and the unnatural darkness of Satis House. The contrast created between the images of light and darkness symbolizes the optimism of prospects and expectations, and the hidden mysteries and scheming that surround Pip as he struggles towards maturity.

Fire and light

Fire is an image that we largely associate with Joe. The warmth of home and hearth, Joe's honest labour, and the forge are inextricably bound together. However, its destructive force, and perhaps to an extent a purifying force, is seen when Miss Havisham burns in her wedding dress.

Light images appear in the novel often in conjunction with mist and shadow which suggests bright fortune but hidden schemes. Frequently the mists rise to disclose sunlight, an image suggesting optimism. There are many images of artificial light, from Estella's candle to the gas lights of the city; and, of course, the star image is associated with Estella, attractive to the eye with its promise of warmth and light yet, in reality, so distant and cold.

Home

Each home depicted in the novel helps to clarify for us the nature of those who live in it. Look, for example, at the symbolism contained in Wemmick's drawbridge. It represents the total distinction he makes between his home and the world outside, particularly the world of work. What do we know of Matthew Pocket's home, of Miss Havisham's, of Mrs Joe's, of Jaggers', of Pip's lodgings, and what do they say about those who live in them? There are very few characters of any note in the story whose homes we do not 'visit' at one time or another.

Relationships

Isolation

Human isolation figures in the novel through each character who suffers in this way either through circumstance, like young Pip, or choice (Miss Havisham) or need (Wemmick and Jaggers). The reader is often made more keenly aware of the specific form of isolation through Dickens's description of their settings.

Love

A whole range of attitudes and responses to love are seen in the novel. We have Pip's love for Estella, paralleled by the love of Herbert and Clara, Wemmick and Miss Skiffins, and Joe and Biddy. Joe's love for Pip finds its reflections in the love given to Pip by Magwitch, Herbert and, eventually, Miss Havisham. However, perhaps the most startling lack of love in the characters' lives is seen in the number of them who are orphans or who do not know who their parents are. Apart from Pip and Estella, which other characters find themselves in this situation?

Atmosphere

Dickens's descriptive mastery can be observed in his settings. The landscape in this novel changes as Pip moves from the misty marshes and village of his childhood, up river to London, the capital city. Pip waits for his expectations to flower in settings which are generally depressing. Note how his fortunes also seem to follow the ebb and flow of the River Thames: the river brings Magwitch to Pip, drowns Compeyson and sees the source of Magwitch's death.

The descriptive powers of Dickens are seen at their best as he recreates the marshes, river and city landscape which so much set the atmosphere which surrounds the slowly changing and maturing Pip. The marsh, with its mists and uncertainties reflects the mood of Pip's early childhood. It is only when Pip has come to terms with himself that he can finally return to the misty wastes of his childhood and come to terms with the marsh.

How would you describe the atmosphere and effect on the reader of Satis House, Wemmick's 'castle', Joe's forge and Mrs Joe's hearth? What is the feeling you get from Jaggers' office and the two courtroom scenes? They all form part and parcel of the author's skill in conveying his feelings and intentions, and the sensitive reader will have his emotions stirred by them as well as wanting to use his intelligence to analyse their effects.

Analysis chart

Important events (listed by chapter where they first appear):

- Ch 1 — Pip aged about 7 years; Pip meets Magwitch.
- Ch 5 — Magwitch & Compeyson recaptured
- Ch 8 — Pip's first acquaintance with Miss Havisham & Estella
- Ch 10 — The stranger at the 'Three Jolly Bargemen'
- Ch 11 — Satis House. Pip fights Herbert Pocket
- Ch 13 — Pip aged about 14 years; Pip apprenticed to Joe.
- Ch 15 — Mrs Joe attacked
- Ch 18 — Pip aged about 18 years; Jaggers announces Pip's 'great expectations'
- Ch 19 — End of first stage of Pip's story
- Ch 20 — Pip leaves for London – meets Wemmick
- Ch 21 — Barnards Inn. Pip & Herbert meet again

	Chapter	1	2	3	4	5	6	7	8	9	10	11	12	13	14	15	16	17	18	19	20	21	22
Places	Joe's house & forge		●		●		●	●		●	●		●		●	●	●	●	●	●			
	Satis House								●			●	●	●		●				●			
	The marsh & river	●		●		●	●									●							
	Pip's lodgings Barnard's Inn & Garden Court																					●	●
	Jaggers' office & house																				●		
	Matthew Pocket's house																						●
	Wemmick's house																						
	Richmond, Pumblechook's house / Wopsle's house / Public houses, Newgate, Clara's house										●			●		●			●	●			
Characters	Pip	●	●	●	●	●	●	●	●	●	●	●	●	●	●	●	●	●	●	●	●	●	●
	Estella								●			●	●			●							
	Magwitch	●		●		●					●												
	Miss Havisham								●	●		●	●	●		●							●
	Joe		●		●	●	●	●		●				●		●			●	●			
	Mrs Joe		●		●								●										
	Biddy							●										●					
	Herbert											●										●	●
	Matthew																						●
	Jaggers												●						●		●		
	Wemmick																					●	
	Molly																						
	Compeyson																						
	Drummle																						
	Orlick															●	●						
	Pumblechook			●	●			●	●										●				
	Trabb's boy																						
	Wopsle				●						●												
Themes	Atmosphere	●		●		●			●													●	
	Expectations			●	●				●	●	●		●	●	●	●	●	●	●		●	●	●
	Imagery	●	●		●				●	●			●										●
	Relationships	●																		●	●		
	Social aspects					●			●	●		●			●				●			●	
	Structure	●	●	●	●	●			●	●	●	●	●		●	●			●				●
	Page in commentary on which chapter first appears	19	20	21	22	23	23	24	24	26	27	27	28	29	29	29	30	30	31	31	32	32	33

Great Expectations — chapter/event chart

Ch.	Event
23	Pip meets Drummle at Matthew Pocket's house
24	Pip's first visit to Walworth
25	Pip meets Molly, at Jaggers' house
26	Joe visits Pip
27	Coach journey with the convicts
28	
29	Herbert announces his engagement to Clara
30	
31	
32	Wemmick shows Pip around Newgate
33	
34	Mrs Joe's death announced
35	Pip aged 21 years.
36	Pip's allowance.
37	Herbert's future secured by Pip's generosity
38	Estella & Miss Havisham argue
39	Magwitch returns.
40	
41	Pip aged 23 years. Second stage ends
42	Magwitch relates his story. They learn Compeyson was Miss Havisham's lover
43	
44	Pip confronts Miss Havisham
45	
46	Compeyson follows Pip
47	Pip realizes Molly is Estella's mother
48	
49	Fire at Satis House
50	Pip realizes Magwitch is Estella's father
51	
52	
53	Orlick attacks Pip
54	Magwitch captured. Compeyson drowns
55	Wemmick marries
56	Magwitch dies
57	Pip ill. Nursed by Joe
58	Biddy & Joe married
59	Passage of 11 years. Pip & Estella reunited

Chapter numbers (top row):
23 24 25 26 27 28 29 30 31 32 33 34 35 36 37 38 39 40 41 42 43 44 45 46 47 48 49 50 51 52 53 54 55 56 57 58 59

Pip's age (bottom row):
34 34 35 35 36 36 37 39 40 40 40 41 42 43 43 44 44 45 46 47 47 49 49 49 50 50 50 51 51 52 52 53 54 54 54 55 55

Finding your way around the commentary

Each page of the commentary gives the following information:

1 A quotation from the start of each paragraph on which a comment is made, or act/scene or line numbers plus a quotation, so that you can easily locate the right place in your text.

2 A series of comments, explaining, interpreting, and drawing your attention to important incidents, characters and aspects of the text.

3 For each comment, headings to indicate the important characters, themes, and ideas dealt with in the comment.

4 For each heading, a note of the comment numbers in this guide where the previous or next comment dealing with that heading occurred.

Thus you can use this commentary section in a number of ways.

1 Turn to that part of the commentary dealing with the chapter/act you are perhaps revising for a class discussion or essay. Read through the comments in sequence, referring all the time to the text, which you should have open before you. The comments will direct your attention to all the important things of which you should take note.

2 Take a single character or topic from the list on page 17. Note the comment number next to it. Turn to that comment in this guide, where you will find the first of a number of comments on your chosen topic. Study it, and the appropriate part of your text to which it will direct you. Note the comment number in this guide where the next comment for your topic occurs and turn to it when you are ready. Thus, you can follow one topic right through your text. If you have an essay to write on a particular character or theme just follow the path through this guide and you will soon find everything you need to know!

3 A number of relevant relationships between characters and topics are listed on page 17. To follow these relationships throughout your text, turn to the comment indicated. As the previous and next comment are printed at the side of each page in the commentary, it is a simple matter to flick through the pages to find the previous or next occurrence of the relationship in which you are interested.

For example, you want to examine in depth the imagery of the novel. Turning to the single topic list, you will find that 'imagery' first occurs in comment 11. On turning to comment 11 you will discover a zero (0) in the place of the previous reference (because this is the first time that it has occurred) and the number 12 for the next reference. You now turn to comment 12 and find that the previous comment number is 11 (from where you have just been looking) and that the next reference is to comment 13, and so on throughout the text.

You also wish to trace the relationship between Pip and Estella throughout the novel. From the relationships list, you are directed to comment 46. This is the first time that both Pip and Estella are discussed together and you will find that the next time that this happens occurs in comment 47 (the 'next' reference for both Pip and Estella). On to comment 47 and you will now discover that two different comment numbers are given for the subject under examination – numbers 49 and 48. This is because each character and idea is traced separately as well as together and you will have to continue tracing them separately until you finally come to comment 60 – the next occasion on which both Pip and Estella are discussed.

Comment number

Quote from novel

Previous appearance in guide

Character or idea under discussion

8 'Hold your noise!'
The convict's appearance and his bloodthirsty threats are not calculated to endear him to either the reader's or Pip's heart. In a sense, the threatening landscape has produced the monster which the 'distant savage lair' threatened, and Pip's worst fears are realized.

0/9   Magwitch
5/12   Atmosphere

Next appearance in guide

Commentary

Single topics:

	Comment no:			Comment no:
Atmosphere	2		Herbert	61
Expectations	18		Matthew	95
Imagery	11			
Relationships	3		Jaggers	58
Social aspects	30		Wemmick	88
Structure	9		Molly	110
Pip	1		Compeyson	188
Estella	39		Drummle	104
Magwitch	8		Orlick	70
Miss Havisham	35			
			Pumblechook	22
Joe	13		Trabb's boy	136
Mrs Joe	13		Wopsle	113
Biddy	32			

Relationships:

			Comment no:
Pip	and	Estella	46
	and	Joe	13
	and	Magwitch	9
	and	Miss Havisham	35
	and	Mrs Joe	13
	and	Biddy	32
	and	Herbert	90
	and	Jaggers	58
	and	Wemmick	102
	and	Expectations	18
	and	Relationships	3
Joe	and	Mrs Joe	13
	and	Miss Havisham	66
	and	Biddy	115
Estella	and	Miss Havisham	46
Expectations	and	Joe	52
	and	Miss Havisham	59
	and	Magwitch	173

Commentary

Chapter 1

1 I gave Pirrip . . .
This introduction to Pip's background presents for us the depressing picture
of his origins; he is an orphan who has effectively christened himself – Pip.
What is a 'pip'? How appropriate is it as a name for the central character,
here aged seven, whom we shall watch grow to maturity?

0/2   Pip

2 Ours was the . . .
Pip's early impression of 'the identity of things' extends to a search for his
own identity in the long sentence beginning 'At such a time . . .'. This
search underlies Pip's striving to become a gentleman. The bleakness of the
landscape helps to emphasize the mood created by our knowledge of Pip's
equally bleak past. When considering the 'identity of things' you also ought
to bear in mind those many occasions in the novel when the appearances of
people and events do not always match up to their reality.

1/3   Pip
0/4   Atmosphere

3 Ours was the . . .
Pip's isolation is stressed in this first view of the marsh and the repetition,
but this time with names, of the long list of his dead brothers, mother and
father.

2/4   Pip
0/76   Relationships

4 Ours was the . . .
Pip feels threatened by the landscape. The references to the 'low leaden
line', which is the river, and to the 'distant savage lair', which is the sea,
between them foreshadow the appearance of the frightening 'monster' who,
literally, will shortly turn Pip's life upside down.

3/6   Pip
2/5   Atmosphere

5 Ours was the . . .
The marsh is an important image in the novel. At this moment it is not a
place that Pip finds easy to come to terms with. Its appearance is unfriendly
and threatening, and totally supports the grim mood of the novel's opening.

4/8   Atmosphere

6 'Hold your noise!'
It does not take much imagination on the reader's part to realize the
frightening effect on Pip of the convict's sudden appearance. This small
child who is totally overawed and frightened by the circumstances in which
he finds himself, and starting to cry from his sheer mental and physical
desolation, is further frightened half to death by the sudden appearance of
the convict.

4/7   Pip

7 'Hold your noise!'
At the start of this novel Pip is just 'a small bundle of shivers'. As the story

6/9   Pip

develops, be aware of the stages that Pip passes through on his way to becoming the mature businessman we see at the end of the novel.

8 'Hold your noise!'

The convict's appearance and his bloodthirsty threats are not calculated to endear him to either the reader's, or Pip's heart. In a sense, the threatening landscape has produced the monster which the 'distant savage lair' threatened, and Pip's worst fears are realized.

0/9	Magwitch
5/12	Atmosphere

9 A fearful man, . . .

Despite the sudden and fearful appearance of the convict, the true personality of the man starts to come through during the subsequent conversation. The grim humour which accompanies his inquisition of Pip to a certain extent belies his terrifying appearance and threats. It helps to relieve the depressing opening of the story and at the same time presents a tremendous contrast in characterization between him and Pip.

7/10	Pip
8/10	Magwitch
0/10	Structure

10 'Blacksmith, eh?' said he.

The fortuitous nature of Joe's profession enables the story to develop smoothly. Pip will now get his first instructions to fulfil the convict's desires, resulting in lies to Joe and theft from his sister. Later, in unknowingly fulfilling his second set of desires, Pip will find himself rejecting Joe in a deeply hurtful and selfish way.

9/11	Pip
9/11	Magwitch
9/12	Structure

11 At the same time . . .

The image of the convict 'eluding the hands of dead people' is prophetic in that he will spend much of the time trying to escape those who would like to see him dead. It also introduces the image of hands, something of which Pip seems very conscious. Be aware of how it provides a thread which connects many of the people in Pip's struggle through to manhood.

10/13	Pip
10/19	Magwitch
0/12	Imagery

12 The marshes were . . .

Note the stark imagery of a landscape reduced to thin red and black lines. Do they suggest darkness and blood? Certainly the gibbet with the convict limping towards it has a powerful suggestion of impending doom. Look out for occasions when another major character is associated with an image of hanging. Be aware that there are a number of events which are repeated or duplicated in one form or another throughout the novel, helping to provide strong structural links.

8/18	Atmosphere
11/13	Imagery
10/17	Structure

Chapter 2

13 My sister, Mrs Joe Gargery, . . .

The description 'by hand' usually implies great care and love, but in Mrs Joe's case it means the very opposite. The imagery which we just saw applied to the convict is now repeated for Pip, not so ominous in its meaning but totally unwelcome by a young lad like him. The first reference of her attitude towards Joe makes one wonder what sort of a man he is—a blacksmith 'brought up by hand'! Note Pip's assessment of Joe in the next

11/16	Pip
0/15	Joe
0/14	Mrs Joe
12/15	Imagery

paragraph 'foolish, dear fellow'. Is this a child's assessment – and, if so, does your view of him need to be a little more perceptive? Note the description of Joe and see to what extent it can be justified by later events in the story.

14 My sister, Mrs Joe, . . .
It would appear that Mrs Joe's character is immediately and totally revealed to us. Does she develop or change at all during the story? Note that nowhere is any impression given of motherliness – the pins and needles at her bib are hardly a comforting place to lay one's head – or real wifely qualities. Does the lack of a Christian or first name perhaps suggest a lack of Christian spirit?

13/16   Mrs Joe

15 Joe's forge adjoined . . .
As you read the novel note the warmth of spirit that is typical of Joe. The forge and his fireside seat in the cottage are images of the strength and security that Pip finds in the company of Joe. Look in this chapter for the many examples of the bond which exists between Joe and Pip, and which serve to highlight the very cruel way in which Pip treats Joe later in the novel.

13/21   Joe
13/21   Imagery

16 By this time, . . .
Mrs Joe's exceedingly rough treatment of Joe and her verbal abuse of him leave us in no doubt as to the ferocity of her temper, and should serve to help us imagine Pip's 'quality' of life at her hands. You must also by now have a reaction to Joe! Can you quantify and justify it? Will you change your mind as you read on?

13/18   Pip
14/26   Mrs Joe

17 There was a door . . .
The end of this chapter, which also denotes the end of the first part of the serialized version of *Great Expectations*, finishes on a note of suspense as Pip makes for the marshes and his date with the convict.

12/20   Structure

Chapter 3

18 The mist was heavier . . .
Note how the landscape seems to reflect the guilt that lies heavily on Pip's conscience. It is interesting that this sense of guilt will stay with Pip for much of the story. You should be aware of the gradual stages by which he comes to terms with his actions and the guilt that attaches to them.

16/19   Pip
12/27   Atmosphere
0/21   Expectations

19 'I think you have . . .'
Does the polite tone of the conversation help to balance the previous frightening meeting between Pip and the convict and show the latter in a quite different light? Is he now seen as someone the reader could pity?

18/20   Pip
11/20   Magwitch

20 'Where is he?'
Magwitch's response to the news of the other convict is rather startling. It certainly suggests that there is no love lost between them and raises the possibility of a mystery which at some later stage will need explaining. It also provides a diversion which allows Pip to slip off into the mist and return home.

19/21	Pip
19/28	Magwitch
17/25	Structure

Chapter 4

21 My sister having so much . . .
In wearing their best clothes for church and the Christmas dinner both Joe and Pip are totally uncomfortable. The 'Sunday penitentials' and 'a kind of reformatory' highlight their discomfort and how much the clothes hide their true personalities. Apart from reflecting on the strictness of life with Mrs Joe note that later in the story both Pip and Joe 'struggle' into clothes which they find uncomfortable – Pip at Trabb's place and Joe when he comes up to London, and later at the funeral. Do they (and especially Pip) feel that being a gentleman is related, somehow, to the clothes they wear?

20/23	Pip
15/23	Joe
18/22	Expectations
15/34	Imagery

22 Mr Wopsle, the clerk . . .
Our first view of Wopsle and Pumblechook in this and the following paragraphs should be noted carefully. Wopsle, with the hints here of his aspirations to greater things, will unintentionally parody Pip's aspirations, but, unlike Pip, Wopsle does not seem to be able to learn from his experiences. How does Pumblechook present himself? Is he really so bountiful in his gifts to Mrs Joe, or is he just indulging his desire to be the centre of attention?

0/24	Pumblechook
0/55	Wopsle
21/24	Expectations

23 Among this good . . .
Pip's share of the abundant dinner illustrates the guests' unfeeling attitude towards the young boy. How does Joe try to improve things for Pip?

21/25	Pip
21/30	Joe

24 I couldn't keep . . .
Pumblechook's cruel insensitivity towards Pip at dinner will shortly get its just reward! His social pretensions (note for example the affected way he prepares to drink his brandy) reflect that theme of snobbery which will later taint Pip in his relationship with Joe.

22/26	Pumblechook
22/36	Expectations

25 My sister went . . .
The terror which Pip feels as Mrs Joe goes to get the pork pie seems to be as great, if not more so, than that which he felt in the presence of the convict. The dinner scene then, is both humorous and dramatic; the chapter ends with Pip's terrified flight to the door and with his being confronted by his worst fears – retribution in the shape of soldiers and a pair of handcuffs seemingly meant for him. It is also the end of the second serial instalment!

23/30	Pip
20/28	Structure

Chapter 5

26 'Missus,' returned the . . .
Obviously a very good judge of character and appearance, notice how over the next few paragraphs the sergeant is immediately able to get on the best side of both Mrs Joe and Pumblechook by the diplomatic use of a little flattery. Their simpering responses should further warn us as to the shallowness of their characters.

27 We were joined . . .
Notice the contrast between the warmth of the home and the forge with the cold, miserable marshland where the convicts are. It will be some time before we see Pip's convict in anything approaching a comfortable situation. Note how at the end of two paragraphs on we see the repetition of those threatening images which we associate with the marsh and now with the convict.

28 Water was splashing, . . .
The reasons for the hostility between the two convicts is not explained, nor why one of the convicts should want to 'give up' the other at the expense of being caught himself. This is particularly intriguing as Magwitch obviously went hunting for the second convict only after Pip had told him of the second escape, and it was done in preference to securing his own safety. We have already mentioned that one scene often finds its reflection further on in the novel. This very fight will find its fulfilment on a later occasion, but in much deeper water.

29 'Lookee here!' said my convict . . .
The episode of the convicts is surely not just a piece of local 'colour'. The obvious hatred in which the other convict is held and the reference to a determination not to let him 'make a tool of me afresh and again' provides us with a mystery which will need to be unravelled.

30 My convict never . . .
It seems to be at this stage that Pip's convict makes a decision that will have tremendous consequences for Pip. The first result of that decision is his exoneration of Pip from the theft of food and the file. Notice Joe's humanity, 'poor miserable fellow-creatur'. His acceptance of the convict as a 'fellow' is in marked contrast to the way they are treated in the boat where they are growled at 'as if to dogs'. The treatment of criminals is a theme which will be turned to at a later stage in the novel; suffice here to note the grimness of the hulks and the attitude of the captors. The convict episode is, temporarily, at an end, and we also come to the end of the third serial instalment.

Chapter 6

31 My state of mind . . .
Pip does not confide in Joe. Can you think why not? Do you consider this the first indication of the gap that grows between them in the novel?

Characters and ideas previous/next comment	
16/65	Mrs Joe
24/36	Pumblechook
18/41	Atmosphere
20/29	Magwitch
25/29	Structure
28/30	Magwitch
28/30	Structure
25/31	Pip
23/31	Joe
29/56	Magwitch
0/32	Social aspects
29/34	Structure
30/32	Pip
30/33	Joe

Chapter 7

32 Mr Wopsle's great-aunt, besides keeping . . .
The lack of educational opportunities and the casual nature of such provision as was made are seen here. Note the detail which Pip gives us in our first view of this other orphan, Biddy. He seems more concerned to concentrate on her appearance than on what she does for him in the way of helping him to learn to read. It foreshadows the mistakes he will make later in the novel when he seems much more concerned with external appearances than internal worth. It is Biddy who, through her teaching, helps him to take the first steps towards being an educated man. Later she will also comment on his 'moral' development, where he needs as much guidance (especially with regard to his obligations towards Joe) as he does with his reading.

33 'Well, Pip,' said Joe, . . .
The history which Joe relates shows us yet another 'fatherless' character. More particularly, it reveals something of the social conditions of the time and begins to give us something of a perspective with which to view Joe and his actions, especially with regard to Mrs Joe and Pip. Carefully study these next few pages where Joe explains something of the underlying reasons and philosophy which guide his actions. You will have a much better understanding of him if you do, especially of his moral strength – something which Pip singularly lacks in the first two stages of the novel.

34 Joe made the fire . . .
Note how Pip views the stars at the end of this paragraph. As you read the story be aware of how closely this view of them mirrors the plan that Miss Havisham has for Estella and those who will be attracted by her beauty.

35 I had heard . . .
When you get to know Miss Havisham's story, you will recognize a certain ironic truth in the description given here.

36 'No, Joseph,' said my sister, . . .
Mr Pumblechook's part in gaining a place for Pip at Miss Havisham's is one he will not let Pip forget. However, perhaps more importantly, the idea of Pip making his fortune through Miss Havisham is planted in Pip's subconscious, preparing the way for those coincidences and deceptions which will confirm him in his belief that she is his benefactor.

37 I had never parted . . .
Episode four ends on a note of mystery and suspense. Exactly why is Pip to go to Miss Havisham's? The reason advanced so far just doesn't make sense – or does it?

Chapter 8

38 Mr Pumblechook and I . . .
The reference to 'mortifying and penitential character' in relation to food and the young is a theme that occurs in other novels by Dickens; the obvious

Characters and ideas	
previous/next comment	
31/35	Pip
0/76	Biddy
30/33	Social aspects
31/36	Joe
32/38	Social aspects
21/41	Imagery
30/37	Structure
32/37	Pip
0/41	Miss Havisham
33/52	Joe
26/38	Pumblechook
24/40	Expectations
35/38	Pip
34/40	Structure
37/41	Pip
36/39	Pumblechook

example is in *Oliver Twist*. You will recall how Pip was previously treated by Pumblechook at the Christmas dinner.

33/45	Social aspects

39 'Oh!' she said.

Why is Pumblechook's dismissal at the gate very satisfying to the reader? However, be aware of the aloofness and coldness of this girl who is roughly the same age as Pip. Could you imagine him being able to dismiss Pumblechook so easily? Quite obviously the girl has had rather a different upbringing from Pip.

0/43	Estella
38/84	Pumblechook

40 'Enough House,' said I; . . .

Is there an implied comment here on the assumption that money can buy everything? As we explore the house in Pip's company we soon come to see that whilst the shell of the building is impressively large, it has no 'heart'. Equally, its owner is in the same condition and even her name – a pun on 'having' and 'sham' – reflects not only the condition of the building she lives in but also her own physical and psychological condition. In terms of wealth she has everything, but what has it bought her?

36/50	Expectations
37/44	Structure

41 She was dressed . . .

As we read this paragraph there is no hint of the terrible reality that lies behind the scene Pip describes. The next paragraph brings us down to earth and speaks of the reality. Note the extraordinary state of Miss Havisham's clothing. To the perceptive reader it must say a great deal about the state of her mind.

38/46	Pip
35/42	Miss Havisham
27/49	Atmosphere
34/42	Imagery

42 It was not . . .

The comparison of Miss Havisham to a waxwork and a skeleton fore-shadows her fate but also comments on her current state. Note the ominous references, 'grave-clothes', 'a shroud', 'corpse-like', here and on subsequent pages, and the associated images of darkness and decay that surround her. Is there any suggestion that she has anything really worthwhile to offer Pip?

41/46	Miss Havisham
41/43	Imagery

43 To stand in the dark . . .

The name Estella means star and she is described thus as she comes, candle in hand, down the dark passage. The comment made in the previous chapter about how Pip saw in the stars 'no help or pity' finds some of its fulfilment anticipated in the next few lines when Miss Havisham reveals her twisted intentions by the words 'break his heart'.

39/45	Estella
42/47	Imagery

44 It was then I began . . .

Notice the blend of Dickens's realism and vigorous imagination in this chapter. He portrays Miss Havisham as a macabre and melodramatic figure in the darkened mansion, who casts her blighting spell on Pip through the cold beauty of Estella. Be aware of the 'fairy-tale' style of presentation; we are not that far from the traditional wicked witch, young hero, sleeping beauty and enchanted palace.

40/53	Structure

45 'With this boy!'

Estella's social contempt for Pip not only says something about Estella and the way Miss Havisham has taught her, but also reflects prevailing social attitudes towards the poor and uneducated. Note how in subsequent

43/46	Estella
38/47	Social aspects

paragraphs she will criticize almost every aspect of Pip. Be aware how much he takes these comments to heart and how they reflect on Pip's view of himself, his home, and Joe.

46 'And never see her again, . . .'

In this chapter Miss Havisham begins to take pleasure in watching Estella hurt Pip. Do we yet know why?

41/47	Pip
45/47	Estella
42/49	Miss Havisham

47 She came back, . . .

Estella gives Pip his food as if he were a disgraced dog; again you can make links with other meals Pip has had. Here he is given enough food but suffers social rejection. From now until the end of the chapter Pip spends much time in an analysis of himself and his life. His assessments here that he was 'morally timid and very sensitive', and in the last paragraph of the chapter that he was a 'common labouring boy' in a 'low-lived bad way' set the scene for the beginning of his rejection of Joe and all he stands for. Be aware of how Pip worries about his appearance, a theme that is constantly returned to.

46/49	Pip
46/48	Estella
43/48	Imagery
45/54	Social aspects

48 Behind the furthest . . .

Note the reference to Estella's appearance at the end of this paragraph. Be aware of how Pip is gradually making her into his 'fairy princess', totally ignoring the reality of how she treats him and all it reveals about her.

47/60	Estella
47/49	Imagery

49 It was in this place, . . .

Pip sees an illusion: a hanging figure of Miss Havisham in the old brewery. As with so many other events and images, this one will be repeated later in the novel. Note how the image reflects the gibbet that the convict moved towards when Pip first left him, and remember this image when you learn more about the fate which almost overtook Estella's real mother – the convict's wife! The images with their complicated associations give an underlying and unobtrusive structural strength to the narrative.

47/50	Pip
46/59	Miss Havisham
41/89	Atmosphere
48/59	Imagery

50 She laughed contemptuously, . . .

Whether he likes it or not, Pip is now effectively launched upon the path he will follow through the novel: his love for Estella and his aspiration to be equal to her, both socially and culturally. Thus the fifth episode ends.

49/51	Pip
40/52	Expectations

Chapter 9

51 When I reached home, . . .

The inquisition that one meets at home after a new experience is something we have all probably experienced, but for Pip that process was a very painful one. The tale he tells is quite fantastic, but is it any less so than the one that actually happened? Is the key to his lies a subconscious desire to shield Estella and her rudeness? Notice also how the insulting treatment he received from Estella is translated into her serving cake and wine on a gold plate! Does his story give us an inkling of the disquieting effect that Estella has had on him?

50/52	Pip

52 'It's a terrible thing, Joe; . . .'
Pip confesses to Joe that he has lied, and one can but laugh at Joe's desperate desire to find that at least one dog, if only a puppy, was there to redeem Pip's lies. The unsettling effect of his visit to Satis House is plain to see, but Joe is quite certain of the value of his advice 'if you can't get to be oncommon by going straight, you'll never get to do it by going crooked'. The seeds of snobbishness have been sown in Pip's mind; he now sees his home and Joe through Estella's eyes.

53 That was a memorable . . .
Notice the presence of the narrator here in the phrase 'Pause you who read this'. Can you understand what it is that the reader is expected to realize at this stage in the novel? What is it that has so affected Pip, and what will it drive him into the world to seek?

Chapter 10

54 The Educational scheme . . .
Biddy is induced to help Pip 'get on in life'. Here is a description of what was known as a 'dame-school' in Victorian England. Notice Pip's realism in the next paragraph, 'it appeared to me . . .', and the fact that, despite it, he determines to persevere with his plan to be properly educated.

55 It being Saturday night . . .
Wopsle is present at the inn when the stranger meets Pip. Notice his interpretation of the Shakespearian passage and the way this foreshadows his attempt to act professionally later in this novel.

56 'You was saying,' . . .
The stranger communicates with Pip in various ways. Can you identify them and make the connection between this man and the convict that Joe helped? This episode will find a reflection later on when Pip will meet yet another stranger in this same public house. Are we to assume that the convict has, via the stranger, paid his debt of gratitude and will disappear from the story?

Chapter 11

57 There were three ladies . . .
The return to Satis House marks the beginning of the seventh episode in the original serialization of the story. Pip meets the three Pocket ladies and describes them as 'humbugs'. Why? Note also what we learn about Matthew Pocket. What evidence is there here that he has very different standards?

Characters and ideas previous/next comment

51/54	Pip
36/66	Joe
50/57	Expectations
44/56	Structure
52/56	Pip
47/67	Social aspects
22/113	Wopsle
54/58	Pip
30/172	Magwitch
53/57	Structure
52/59	Expectations
56/58	Structure

58 He was a burly man . . .
This chance meeting with the man who will turn out to be Jaggers, Miss Havisham's lawyer, will serve to convince Pip that he knows who his benefactor really is.

59 I crossed the . . .
The centrepiece of the derelict wedding feast is the great cake. It acts as a symbol of those great – and disappointed – expectations which Miss Havisham once had, and in its decaying condition reflects the state of Miss Havisham's mind. Her comment that she will be laid on that table when she is dead will be ironically fulfilled, but it will happen before she dies.

60 She stood looking . . .
The reference to Pip worrying that both he and Estella might 'begin to decay' is rather ironic, given Miss Havisham's plans for them.

61 This pale young gentleman . . .
This introduction to the person we will later discover to be Herbert Pocket provides a welcome relief to the encounters we have had with the various 'toadies', and to the twisted natures of Miss Havisham and Estella. His insistence on rules, his determination, and refusal to accept defeat all begin to reveal some charming character traits. Certainly, it would seem that Pip could learn a few things from him. Consider whether or not Herbert has any 'great' expectations.

62 I kissed her . . .
The kiss which Estella allows Pip to take makes him feel totally worthless. As he returns to his home we see the repetition of the black and red images which accompanied his contacts with the convict in the earlier chapter. Do they suggest the darkness and danger, both moral and physical, which will afflict Pip in the years to come? The fire which the furnace threw across his path seems almost to be a warning to him directly from Joe.

Chapter 12

63 My mind grew . . .
Note the irrational fear that Pip has about the Law coming to punish him for the fight with Herbert. It echoes the guilt he felt over the theft of the file and food, earlier, though at least then there was some justification for his guilty feelings. It is in this confused state that we find him at the beginning of this eighth episode in the serialization. Your attention will not be drawn to any future episodes, but do look out for those occasions where the author has carefully allowed for the serial form of publication.

Characters and ideas
previous/next comment

56/60	Pip
0/79	Jaggers
57/63	Structure
49/64	Miss Havisham
57/64	Expectations
49/60	Imagery
58/62	Pip
48/62	Estella
59/62	Imagery
0/90	Herbert
60/63	Pip
60/64	Estella
60/93	Imagery
62/64	Pip
58/73	Structure

64 As we began . . .
Pip's hopes for greater things through Miss Havisham meet little encouragement from her. Instead it is rather the opposite as she seems much more concerned to learn of the effect that Estella is having on him. Her injunction to Estella, 'Break their hearts . . . no mercy!', is rather ironic in the light of the dispute that she and Estella will have later.

63/66	Pip
62/71	Estella
59/66	Miss Havisham
59/65	Expectations

65 When I got home . . .
Why should Mrs Joe fly into such a rage when Pip brought the news about his indentures? Did she hope Miss Havisham would do rather more for Pip, and therefore for herself?

26/73	Mrs Joe
64/66	Expectations

Chapter 13

66 'You expected,' said Miss Havisham, . . .
Despite the embarrassment that Pip felt about Joe's speaking to him in reply to Miss Havisham's questions, Miss Havisham seems not the least bit put out by it. Note he indicates he did not expect a premium 'with the boy', but gets one nevertheless. This episode will find a reflection in a similar conversation with Jaggers, but with a different outcome. What is Miss Havisham's reaction to Joe? There is a key phrase just after the exchange about the 'premium', and also when she calls him back to talk privately, which shows an astute awareness of character on her part.

64/68	Pip
52/70	Joe
64/71	Miss Havisham
65/68	Expectations

67 The Justices were . . .
This will not be the the last visit Pip makes to a court. Those glimpses we get here of its unsatisfactory nature will be enlarged upon later in the novel.

54/81	Social aspects

Chapter 14

68 It is a most miserable . . .
Pip's view of his home has been changed, and he is bitterly disappointed about being indentured to Joe. What is the 'ungracious condition' of his mind at this stage? Would you say that at this moment some of Miss Havisham's plans have come to fruition?

66/69	Pip
66/69	Expectations

Chapter 15

69 Whatever I acquired, . . .
The fact that Pip has not revealed to Joe that he is unhappy as a blacksmith is one slight redeeming feature of his behaviour. However, note the reasons why he tries to help Joe. His determination to visit Miss Havisham gives us some idea of the desperate frame of mind in which Pip finds himself. It is interesting to contrast the Pip we knew before the visits to Satis House, with the one we see now.

68/70	Pip
68/71	Expectations

Characters and ideas
previous/next comment

70 Now, Joe kept . . .
Orlick is Joe's journeyman (i.e. someone in the final stage of apprenticeship before becoming a master of craft in his own right). Notice the description which establishes his attitudes – he is not a very pleasant character. However, there is nothing wrong with his wit, and he quickly points out to Joe the favouritism of letting Pip off for a half day but not doing the same for 'Old Orlick'. What is it that makes him envious of Pip? What do you think of his comments on Mrs Joe's character?

69/71	Pip
66/80	Joe
0/72	Orlick

71 Everything was unchanged, . . .
Pip clings to his hopes, but Miss Havisham's first words are not spoken lightly; she means every word. Her evident enjoyment at his discomfiture shows she has not changed. Despite Estella being absent, the visit brings back old memories and rekindles his dissatisfaction with life at the forge.

70/72	Pip
64/115	Estella
66/91	Miss Havisham
69/74	Expectations

72 Old Orlick growled, . . .
Orlick's comment that he had followed Pip into town foreshadows the time when he will again do so, but this time to London, and with dangerous intent towards Pip in an attempt to repeat recent criminal actions (in which his involvement will be confirmed at a later date).

71/74	Pip
70/74	Orlick

73 We were running . . .
Mrs Joe meets a sudden, violent attack and suffers a lingering death. Do we feel any pity for her? If not, why not? Notice how her death clears the way for Biddy to move into the house and for her relationship with Joe to develop.

65/154	Mrs Joe
63/74	Structure

Chapter 16

74 With my head full . . .
Yet again Pip feels guilty, this time for the attack on Mrs Joe; it is some measure of the mental turmoil he finds himself in and of the lack of security he feels. You should bear this in mind when making judgments about his character. The mystery of who attacked Mrs Joe must be added to those other mysteries which have yet to be resolved. Can you recall some of them?

72/75	Pip
72/122	Orlick
71/76	Expectations
73/79	Structure

Chapter 17

75 So unchanging was . . .
Note the unremitting hold that the image of Satis House has on Pip.

74/76	Pip

76 'Oh, I wouldn't, . . .'
Does the admiration which Pip expresses for Biddy in the previous and subsequent paragraphs suggest a growing affection for her? If so, it is strangely mixed with insensitivity – can you see how? Note how inward looking Pip is, his every thought is about what *he* wants.

75/77	Pip
32/77	Biddy
74/77	Expectations
3/77	Relationships

77 'If I could have . . .'
Study this conversation carefully for the insight it gives us into the relationships between Pip and Biddy, and Pip's desire for Estella. Biddy's analysis of his reasons for wanting to be a gentleman is particularly interesting. It is a shame Pip cannot learn from it! Do you think his comment about wishing he could get himself to fall in love with her very gentlemanlike?

76/78	Pip
76/78	Biddy
76/82	Expectations
76/78	Relationships

78 'But it makes no difference . . .'
Note Biddy's reaction to Pip's concern about the attention Orlick is paying to her, and what it says about her attitude to Pip.

77/80	Pip
77/112	Biddy
77/82	Relationships

Chapter 18

79 The strange gentleman, . . .
This is the second meeting Pip has had with a stranger in this public house. Can you remember the first one? This duplication of events helps to provide strong structural links in the novel, and in this case could give us a hint as to who really gives Jaggers his instructions in respect of Pip. What indications do we get of Jaggers' character here?

58/80	Jaggers
74/80	Structure

80 'Bear in mind then, . . .'
This is the second time Joe has been quizzed about the 'monetary value' he puts on Pip, and the second time he has responded with dignity. The news that Pip has 'great expectations', told to him from the lips of a man he met at Satis House, convinces Pip, wrongly as it turns out, that Miss Havisham is his benefactress. The strict emphasis on the secrecy that is to surround the source of this money helps to add another mystery to the novel. If Pip is so quickly able to trace the source, why has the author included such an easily discovered 'red herring'?

78/82	Pip
70/85	Joe
79/81	Jaggers
79/94	Structure

81 Correcting myself, I said . . .
Jaggers' determination that Pip should use the absolutely correct words in response to Jaggers' questions reflects his conversation with Wopsle a little while ago. Would you agree that he is only concerned with the absolute letter of the law and not at all with its spirit?

80/86	Jaggers
67/87	Social aspects

82 I never could . . .
Pip prepares to leave home to become a gentleman. Note Pip's feelings as his departure nears, and particularly his growing sense of isolation.

80/83	Pip
77/83	Expectations
78/116	Relationships

Chapter 19

83 After our early dinner . . .
Note the irony of Pip's imagining himself bestowing good food on the villagers and in the next paragraph the feelings he has about the convict – who would indirectly be paying for that food! What does the

82/84	Pip
82/85	Expectations

reference to 'a gallon of condescension' say about Pip's attitude? Look further into the chapter at his conversation with Biddy about Joe's manners, and later his encounter with Trabb's boy. Pip is already out of touch with the reality of life as lived in the marshes – the only reality for Pip now is being a 'gentleman'. The dust that Trabb's boy sweeps over him is perhaps fitting enough comment on the quality of his aspirations at this moment!

84 By degrees he fell to . . .
Contrast the meal Pip is given by Pumblechook with the dinner he received in chapter 4. What does Pumblechook's change of attitude tell us about him? Note also that Pip seems more well disposed towards Pumblechook, especially if you look back at his feelings about the man in earlier chapters. When at Trabb's place, he remarked on the power of money, here he sees its effect on Pumblechook and realizes that it also buys power.

83/85   Pip
39/119 Pumblechook

85 I walked away . . .
Pip did not wish Joe to see him off in the coach, conscious of the 'difference' there was between them. However, there would still seem to be a conflict in his emotions. The mist lifts and for a moment he regains the vision of his lost innocence, and cries. Does the reader feel some sympathy with Pip at this stage for the tremendous conflicts of emotions he is suffering, conflicts which his life hasn't trained him to deal with? Bear this in mind when assessing his character at this stage.

84/86   Pip
80/107 Joe
83/86   Expectations

Chapter 20

86 The journey from . . .
Pip's dream of London and its reality do not match. Note the awe with which the coachman refers to Jaggers, and the unceremonious way in which a client is thrown out of the office, with his hat following him.

85/87   Pip
81/87   Jaggers
85/89   Expectations

87 While I looked . . .
Pip's stroll gives him a slight idea of what London is really like, and a view of the more brutal aspects of the legal system. Note how Jaggers treats those who would be his clients; is there little sense of justice and even less sense of mercy in his dealings with these people?

86/90   Pip
86/101 Jaggers
81/100 Social aspects

Chapter 21

88 Casting my eyes . . .
Note this description of Wemmick and see how well it fits both his public and private life.

0/112   Wemmick

89 There was an air . . .
Notice the contrast between Pip's expectations and the reality. His 'great expectations' have caused him to swop the comfort of life with Joe and Biddy and the open landscape of the marshes, for the narrow city streets and the squalor of Barnard's Inn.

49/109	Atmosphere
86/90	Expectations

90 'Pray come in,' . . .
We immediately see Herbert as one who would not take from his father – he has his 'own bread to earn'; what a sharp contrast he is to Pip. You might like to consider how apt are the two descriptions they give of each other at this very moment.

87/91	Pip
61/91	Herbert
89/92	Expectations

Chapter 22

91 'How did you bear . . .'
Pip cannot comprehend how Herbert could take such a disappointment lightly, which rather underlines the great differences in their characters. Pip's comments in subsequent paragraphs add further emphasis to the differences. Why should Herbert's carefree and open explanations of his family connections with Miss Havisham and Mr Jaggers make Pip feel on 'dangerous ground'?

90/93	Pip
71/94	Miss Havisham
90/92	Herbert

92 As he was so communicative, . . .
Notice Herbert's natural tact and friendliness as he agrees to help improve Pip's manners. He provides an example of what a true gentleman should be.

91/93	Herbert
90/95	Expectations

93 'Would you mind . . .'
How does the nickname Herbert chooses for Pip illustrate Herbert's lack of snobbery? Is 'Harmonious Blacksmith' a good description of Joe? Note also the repetition of the 'hand' image implicit in the new name for Pip.

91/96	Pip
92/94	Herbert
62/99	Imagery

94 'Now,' he pursued, . . .
Carefully read Herbert's account of Miss Havisham's life story. Note those comments about what makes a gentleman, and the money-grabbing nature of most of Miss Havisham's relatives. This account of her story will find its parallel later in the novel with an account of Magwitch's life story.

93/114	Herbert
91/120	Miss Havisham
80/101	Structure

95 'There appeared upon . . .'
How does the comment 'a true gentleman in manner . . . a true gentleman at heart' reveal a fundamental theme of this novel?

0/98	Matthew
92/96	Expectations

96 In truth, he said this . . .
The acceptance by both young men that Miss Havisham is Pip's benefactress helps prop up the structure of illusion that Pip and others have built around him. The reality of the matter will therefore come as an even greater shock.

93/99	Pip
95/97	Expectations

Characters and ideas previous/next comment

Chapter 23

97 I found out within . . .
Note how the humorous account of Mrs Pocket's snobbery caricatures the snobbery which Pip demonstrates at various times.

98 I was made very . . .
The reference to Drummle and Mrs Pocket discussing 'two baronetcies' should perhaps serve as a warning about Drummle; we already know about Mrs Pocket's snobbery. Note some paragraphs on in the chapter how Matthew, despite his strange ways, is much more realistic, as seen in his sarcastic comment 'Are infants to be nutcrackered . . .?'

99 In the evening . . .
Pip's intention to add elegance to his rowing points at his continuing determination to pursue the path of becoming a 'gentleman'. His reaction to the 'arms of a blacksmith' clearly demonstrates how ashamed he now feels of his background, and, by implication, Joe. The introduction of the river is important to the continuing narrative and its image lends a continuity to the events of Pip's life.

Chapter 24

100 After two or . . .
Pip's education is not to include training for any profession because he is destined to be a 'gentleman'. At almost every turn the reader is being encouraged to consider what a gentleman really is. You might like to compare the characters of Matthew and Joe. Both are childlike in some ways, but both are also gentlemen. Does Pip recognize this, at least in so far as Matthew is concerned?

101 'Come!' retorted Mr Jaggers, . . .
Notice Pip's growing confidence, even when confronting the formidable Jaggers. Can you see the small structural link at the beginning of Pip's time in London which is provided by this mathematical question and answer? If you can't, think back to Pip's early visit to Satis House at the start of the story.

102 'Always seems to me,' . . .
The guided tour of Jaggers' establishment is a timely reminder for us of the savage face of justice and the whimsical way of its workings. It also serves to establish friendly relations between Wemmick and Pip which will assist in the furtherance of the narrative.

103 'Well,' said Wemmick, . . .
Wemmick hints at something very strange about Jaggers' housekeeper – 'a wild beast tamed', though at this stage the reader only recognizes this as an illustration of Jaggers' power. Note how even the 'magistrates shivered . . . hung in dread rapture on his words'. Do you think that this is a sign of real justice at work?

Characters and ideas	
previous/next comment	
96/98	Expectations
95/100	Matthew
97/100	Expectations
96/100	Pip
93/108	Imagery
99/101	Pip
98/240	Matthew
98/105	Expectations
87/102	Social aspects
100/102	Pip
87/103	Jaggers
94/110	Structure
101/104	Pip
88/103	Wemmick
100/106	Social aspects
101/108	Jaggers
102/106	Wemmick

Chapter 25

104 Bentley Drummle, who . . .
It is perhaps fortunate that Pip does at the very least seem able to recognize that Drummle is not a pleasant fellow. Pip's friendship with Herbert and Startop does throw some light on his own underlying characteristics – can you see why? (Think about the proverb 'Birds of a feather . . .'!)

105 When I had been in . . .
The influence that Pip's expectations had on others is seen in how the Pockets' hatred for him is suppressed whilst they 'fawn' on him. Is it therefore not surprising that it should have such a profound effect on him?

106 It appeared to be . . .
The description of Wemmick's home and the extraordinary difference between the public and private Wemmick highlight the extremes to be found in society. It also illustrates the need which Wemmick seems to have to preserve a strict barrier between his two lives in order that he himself might survive. The drawbridge is a particularly apt image of this.

107 'Well aged parent,' . . .
There is a nice contrast here between Wemmick's loving care for his 'aged parent' and Pip's treatment of Joe. While the two situations – and the relationships involved – are clearly not the same, would you consider that the underlying concept is the same? Is Wemmick a 'gentleman' – or would your answer depend on whether Wemmick was at the office or at home?

Chapter 26

108 It fell out . . .
Jaggers' habit of handwashing repeats the imagery associated with hands, but does it also imply something about his inner feelings towards his profession?

109 He conducted us . . .
Read the description of Jaggers' home. Do you find it in keeping with his working life?

110 Her entrapped hand . . .
The drawing of our attention to Molly's hands does not tell us anything at the moment, but it is something to which Pip will return at a later stage.

Characters and ideas	
previous/next comment	
102/105	Pip
0/111	Drummle
104/107	Pip
100/113	Expectations
103/107	Wemmick
102/141	Social aspects
105/110	Pip
85/112	Joe
106/161	Wemmick
103/109	Jaggers
99/124	Imagery
108/132	Jaggers
89/123	Atmosphere
107/112	Pip
0/211	Molly
101/118	Structure

111 In our boyish . . .
The dispute between the four young men provides some amusement for
Jaggers, particularly with regard to Drummle. Indeed, at one point near the
end of the chapter Jaggers is almost drawn to make a prediction of
Drummle's future. Given Jaggers' experiences one wonders what sort of
future he sees for him. Also be aware of how the other three display their
characters and note the differences between them.

104/168   Drummle

Chapter 27

112 'P.S. He wishes . . .'
Biddy's P.S. says a great deal about how she thinks Pip might respond to
Joe's wish to visit him in London. She suggests that Pip's 'good heart' will
enable him to overcome the fact that he is a 'gentleman'! Pip is so very
unhappy about the forthcoming visit; what does it say about Biddy's
perception of things that she realizes this? Note also what his reaction says
about his own character at this moment.

110/115   Pip
107/113   Joe
 78/115   Biddy

113 'Had a drop, Joe?'
Joe cannot have missed the pretentious presence of Pip's young 'Avenger' at
the door. Is his opinion that leaving the Church and taking up playacting is a
'drop' for Wopsle also an inference about Pip's 'playacting' as a gentleman?

112/114   Joe
 55/140   Wopsle
105/114   Expectations

114 'When did you . . .'
When Herbert meets Joe, the reader is presented with an example of truly
gentlemanly behaviour. Notice Pip's snobbish thoughts whereas Herbert
has none.

113/115   Joe
 94/138   Herbert
113/117   Expectations

115 'Which I fully believed . . .'
The message from Miss Havisham reintroduces one of the central reasons
that Pip has for wanting to be a gentleman – Estella. A few paragraphs on,
Joe gives one explanation of why Biddy did not include Miss Havisham's
request to see Pip in her letter. Can you deduce another reason?

112/116   Pip
 71/121   Estella
114/116   Joe
112/155   Biddy

116 I had not been . . .
Pip here recognizes that what is important about Joe is not his clothes, but
that the man who wears them has a 'simple dignity'. Perhaps Pip is
beginning to show a greater awareness of the distinction between appearance and reality. Look back to the end of chapter 19 and see how closely
Pip's reaction here is similar to his feelings then. What do the two occasions
say about Pip's underlying feelings for Joe, feelings which his pursuit of the
status of 'gentleman' get in the way of?

115/117   Pip
115/134   Joe
 82/121   Relationships

Chapter 28

117 It was clear . . .
The youthful Pip finds reasons why he should stay at the Blue Boar instead
of the forge. Do you agree that he is a 'self-swindler'?

116/118   Pip
114/119   Expectations

118 At that time . . .
Notice the way Dickens inserts a reminder of Pip's connection with the convicts, particularly Magwitch, just when his future and links with Miss Havisham seem assured. Would you consider that coincidence has been stretched rather too far by the author making one of the convicts the same one that gave Pip the two pounds? However, it does serve to remind the reader about Magwitch and makes us wonder if he will return at some stage.

117/120	Pip
110/120	Structure

119 Our readers will learn . . .
Here is a further example of Pumblechook's pretentiousness. Despite being a reasonably well-off man, Pumblechook only seems able to find satisfaction by taking advantage of others' weaknesses (e.g. of Pip when he was very young) or by pretending to himself that the fortunes of others are largely as a result of his efforts. Along with the Pockets, the Finches and numerous other characters he fills out our view of the false idea of what constitutes a 'gentleman', as well, of course, as providing some humorous interludes.

84/223	Pumblechook
117/120	Expectations

Chapter 29

120 She had adopted . . .
Pip clearly believes that Miss Havisham has grandiose plans for him, and he indulges in a romantic fantasy; remember the comment in the section on 'Understanding *Great Expectations*' about the fairy story aspect of the novel.

118/121	Pip
94/124	Miss Havisham
119/122	Expectations
118/123	Structure

121 She had adopted . . .
Pip is unable, or is it unwilling, to face reality. He holds his love for Estella to be the sole motivating force of his life. These first two paragraphs suggest an immature and totally unrealistic nature. It will need something of a shock, or a series of shocks, to return him to reality.

120/122	Pip
115/124	Estella
116/130	Relationships

122 I so shaped . . .
Would you agree that when Pip turned his back on the door of Satis House his expectation was that when he turned round he would see Estella? What a shock to his expectations then, when not Estella, but Orlick stands in front of him! Despite Pip's learning, he doesn't quite seem to be the match for Orlick when it comes to repartee.

121/123	Pip
74/123	Orlick
120/126	Expectations

123 By this time we had come . . .
Orlick's presence in Satis House reminds the reader of the house's menacing, brooding and dark symbolism. It should help the reader become aware that Pip's hopes cannot be realized through Miss Havisham and her darkened world. There will be a second appearance of Orlick and his gun, but then it will be more than just a threatening presence.

122/124	Pip
122/135	Orlick
109/159	Atmosphere
120/129	Structure

124 She was in her chair . . .
Can you remember when Pip first saw this shoe? Look back to the middle of chapter 8. Now it is in Estella's possession. Is there an implied suggestion here that Estella is now about to take Miss Havisham's revenge? Note also the constant references to hands in this scene with Miss Havisham and Estella.

123/125	Pip
121/125	Estella
120/125	Miss Havisham
108/128	Imagery

125 'Do you find . . .'
Miss Havisham's 'greedy look' illustrates the true nature of her interest in Pip's reaction to meeting Estella again. Do you know what she is interested in here?

124/126	Pip
124/126	Estella
124/130	Miss Havisham

126 'Since your change . . .'
Pip's ready agreement with Estella's assumption that he will have changed his companions since his change of fortunes points to his lack of moral fibre and values, both serious faults in his character. He will need to overcome these failings if he is ever to grow into a true gentleman.

125/127	Pip
125/127	Estella
122/136	Expectations

127 'You must know,' . . .
If Estella has 'no heart' why does she warn Pip of the fact? We see in Pip, on the odd occasion when his better nature shows through, a longing to be at peace with Joe. Could Estella have similar 'problems' which account for this warning?

126/130	Pip
126/128	Estella

128 In another moment . . .
Pip will later be able to put all these 'ghosts' together when he discovers Estella's true identity. The hands will be an important clue for him.

127/130	Estella
124/133	Imagery

129 Her handsome dress . . .
When will this scene of Pip and Estella in the garden be repeated and under what circumstances?

123/136	Structure

130 She drew an arm . . .
Note these words of Miss Havisham and those, a few paragraphs on, when she urges Pip to love Estella, effectively against all reason. Can you remember Pip's description of how he loved Estella, at the beginning of this chapter? Is the love that is urged on him and the love he feels, real 'love'?

127/134	Pip
128/131	Estella
125/131	Miss Havisham
121/134	Relationships

131 'Estella's name. Is it . . .'
Can you remember what Herbert told Pip of Miss Havisham's history? Did he mention Estella? How much does Pip, and the reader, now know about Miss Havisham and Estella? Perhaps more to the point, what is it that Pip really wants to ask Jaggers?

130/132	Estella
130/144	Miss Havisham

132 Anything to equal . . .
Why should Jaggers avoid looking at Estella, but she should often look at him? Is there an unspoken secret between them? Certainly it creates a mystery for Pip, and the reader.

131/133	Estella
109/142	Jaggers

133 I think Miss Pocket . . .
The surrounding of Estella with glittering jewels reminds us of the star image and its inaccessibility.

132/134	Estella
128/150	Imagery

134 Ah me! I thought . . .
Pip admits that Estella keeps him from Joe. The only true companion and real gentleman that Pip had ever known is supplanted by a distant, cold and contemptuous 'star'. What a choice Pip has made!

130/136	Pip
133/138	Estella
116/154	Joe
130/139	Relationships

Chapter 30

135 After well considering . . .
Pip is instrumental in Orlick's dismissal. Later he will have cause, perhaps, to regret the action.

123/157	Orlick

136 Casting my eyes . . .
The hilarious episode, for us but not for Pip, of his encounter with Trabb's boy does nothing to bring him to his senses. Even the constant repetition of 'Don't know yah!' which ought to have reminded Pip of the cruel way he had ignored Joe on this visit leaves Pip untouched. His only thought is for his own dignity. The depths to which he descends are such that he writes to Trabb's employer in an obvious effort to get him dismissed. You will appreciate the irony of this when you consider the later actions of Trabb's boy and those of the other person Pip has caused to be dismissed from a job on this trip to Satis House. If you cannot make the connection, chapter 53 will provide the answer!

134/137	Pip
0/226	Trabb's boy
126/140	Expectations
129/147	Structure

137 'I am ashamed to say it,' . . .
This exchange between Pip and Herbert is interesting because it is one of the rare moments when the problem of what Pip has become is explicitly discussed. Can you make your own assessment at this moment of Pip? When attempting to do so, always remember to look for reasons and justification, not only of your opinions but also of what Pip says and does, both from his point of view as well as yours. Try to understand him, before you judge him. How might you have acted given the same circumstances?

136/141	Pip

138 'Yes; but my dear . . .'
Note Herbert's quite lucid reasoning as to why Pip should give up Estella. Do you agree with him?

134/141	Estella
114/139	Herbert

139 'Oh yes! And so the dustman . . .'
Notice the way the value and reality of Herbert's love for his Clara is established through humour and lack of social pretensions. You might like to compare this with Pip's overpowering, unrealistic compulsion to love, and be socially acceptable to, Estella.

138/151	Herbert
134/146	Relationships

Chapter 31

140 On our arrival . . .
At roughly the centre of the novel, with so many mysteries and loose ends, and with Pip hopelessly in love, we have a large slice of comic relief. Wopsle achieves his desire to play the great, tragic character, Hamlet – not the easiest of Shakespearian roles. He fails, convincingly. How convincingly has Pip failed, so far, to live the life of a true gentleman?

| 113/209 | Wopsle |
| 136/150 | Expectations |

Chapter 32

141 One day when . . .
Note the tremendous contrast between the cold tone of Estella's note and the frantic response of Pip. It takes a visit to the horrors of Newgate to make his mind forget her for a moment. Be aware of how frequently we find events being duplicated in the novel. This is Pip's second visit to Newgate. Can you remember the circumstances of his first? This visit puts a little more flesh on the bare bones of our previous view. Note how the ability to pay for one's defence is the sole criterion of whether or not Wemmick will speak to someone. He sees nothing wrong with accepting gifts from prisoners and even requesting 'portable property' from condemned criminals. How do you react to his actions, and why?

137/143	Pip
138/143	Estella
106/142	Social aspects

142 'Mind you, Mr Pip,' . . .
What sort of reflection on justice and society is it that Jaggers should wield such power over people's 'soul and body'? Do we ever really get to know Jaggers and what motivates him?

| 132/148 | Jaggers |
| 141/152 | Social aspects |

143 Mr Wemmick and I . . .
There is an irony in Pip's desire to rid himself of the air and dust of Newgate so as not to sully the 'proud and refined' Estella. The 'nameless shadow' which he mentions perhaps suggests there is a hidden secret about her past – time will tell, and the telling will illuminate the irony. (Alternatively you could read ahead to chapter 48.)

| 141/146 | Pip |
| 141/145 | Estella |

Chapter 33

144 'I am going to Richmond,' . . .
Note the absolute control which Miss Havisham seems to exert over these two young people. Despite being far from her they comply with her every instruction, even to the extent that Estella puts her arm through Pip's 'as if it must be done'.

| 131/156 | Miss Havisham |

145 'It is not easy . . .'
The conversation just held about the Pocket family and their hatred for Pip gives us a small insight into Estella's life at Satis House. It is ironic that Pip should worry that their lies might do him a disservice in Miss Havisham's

| 143/146 | Estella |

Characters and ideas
previous/next comment

eyes; he has yet to realize that his expectations from that quarter are totally without foundation. Note Estella's reference to 'that impostor of a woman'. Could Estella be referring to Miss Havisham here? Would her comment fit Miss Havisham as we know her to date?

146 I leaned down, . . .
Does Pip debase himself when he kisses Estella's cheek after being allowed to do so? She is as indifferent to this kiss as she was to the first.

143/149	Pip
145/148	Estella
139/149	Relationships

147 The bill paid, . . .
The ridiculous extravagance of the tea urn and accompanying cups provides a comic relief from the intensity of Pip's love for Estella.

136/157	Structure

148 'What place is that?'
The reference to Newgate prison and Estella's reaction, 'Wretches!', her mention of seeing Jaggers 'ever since I can remember', and her obvious dislike of the man are all highly ironic. She seems so far removed from this world of Newgate and Jaggers, yet her very origins, life and fortune are inextricably bound up with them, as we shall see as the story unfolds. Most particularly, note how she shrinks from the thought of visiting his house. Why should this be so ironic?

146/149	Estella
142/160	Jaggers

149 It was impossible . . .
Pip recognizes that Estella is making advances to him, but finds that it does not make him happy. Is his analysis of her attitude totally accurate?

146/150	Pip
148/165	Estella
146/156	Relationships

Chapter 34

150 As I had grown . . .
The recurring guilt which Pip feels about Joe and Biddy resurfaces here. It nags at the back of his mind and perhaps suggests that Pip can be redeemed. Conflicting influences in Pip's life – the warmth and vitality of Joe and the frigid attractions of Estella – are expressed by the opposed imagery of fire and stars throughout the novel.

149/151	Pip
140/151	Expectations
133/171	Imagery

151 Yet Estella was . . .
The lavish life-style of an idle gentleman has no purpose. It leads Pip towards debt and unsettles Herbert.

150/152	Pip
139/164	Herbert
150/153	Expectations

152 So now, as an . . .
Membership of The Finches of the Grove will lead Pip into even greater excesses and highlight the Victorian view of what a 'gentleman' was.

151/154	Pip
142/153	Social aspects

153 We spent as much . . .
Until the end of this chapter we are regaled with the picture of Herbert and
Pip getting further and further into debt. Both become depressed and only
revive their flagging spirits by doing their bookkeeping in such a way as to
pretend they have money to spare; they are comforted by the thought of
their 'margin'. Both of them are moving away from the reality of things, but
the more they move away the closer they bring themselves to the reality of
Jaggers' world and the debtors' prison. Why do you think they cannot see
this?

151/158	Expectations
152/154	Social aspects

Chapter 35

154 Whatever my fortunes . . .
Pip's response to Mrs Joe's death is 'regret' without 'tenderness'. Notice the
way the sunshine and summer landscape at the funeral 'softens the edge' of
his childhood fears of her. The funeral is made into an occasion of
pretentiousness by onlookers and participants alike. The Hubbles and
Pumblechook are more concerned with their own appearance and that of
others to be seriously thinking of Mrs Joe. Only Joe seems to be really upset
by the event and when he voices the opinion that he would have preferred
to carry her to church himself, he cuts through all the social pretensions and
we see a truly gentle man. Don't ignore the large vein of humour that runs
through this account by which the author pokes fun at the ridiculous antics
of Trabb and his cohorts.

152/155	Pip
134/159	Joe
73/156	Mrs Joe
153/187	Social aspects

155 'Biddy,' said I, . . .
The suggestion that Biddy ought to have written to Pip receives a dusty
answer from her. If Pip had been a true gentleman, one might have
supposed he would have bothered, from time to time, to enquire after his
sister's health! Insensitive as ever, Pip offers her money, but fails to realize
that Biddy has changed from the girl he once knew into a mature woman.
Her thoughts on his becoming a gentleman are obvious enough for us to
perceive that she would not take money *from* Pip, no more than Joe would
take money from Jaggers, *for* him.

154/156	Pip
115/223	Biddy

156 'They are very slight, . . .'
What would appear to be a deathbed repentance on Mrs Joe's part, when
she asks for Joe's and Pip's pardon, will find a parallel in a similar scene with
Miss Havisham. Both women had a great influence on Pip's life; Mrs Joe, in a
negative and punitive way, deprives him of love and comfort in his
childhood, and Miss Havisham gives him expectations which she believes
(wrongly as it turns out) he could never attain. Do you think both women
repent for the same reason, that they ultimately recognized the wrong they
had done? Additionally, has Miss Havisham's repentance something to do
with a growing respect for Pip?

155/158	Pip
144/166	Miss Havisham
154/0	Mrs Joe
149/163	Relationships

157 'Do you know what . . .'
The reference to Orlick and his threatening presence serves as a timely
reminder that his part in the story is yet to be unfolded.

135/194	Orlick
147/170	Structure

158 'Are you quite sure, . . .'
What do you think of Biddy's remark and Pip's response? Is she right in her judgment that Pip's words mean very little? Is he totally deluding himself when he suggests that he is shocked by her assessment of his character? What evidence would you refer to in order to justify either point of view?

156/159	Pip
153/160	Expectations

159 Early in the morning, . . .
It is appropriate at this point that we should see Joe in bright light and sunshine, perhaps reflecting the future which lies in store for him. Pip is shrouded in mist which foreshadows his future sorrows and uncertainties.

158/160	Pip
154/223	Joe
123/171	Atmosphere

Chapter 36

160 'This is a bank-note,' . . .
Pip comes of age and is informed that he has £500 a year on which to live. Jaggers shows himself very much aware of Pip's life-style and attitudes, but expresses no opinions on the matter – which is totally in keeping with the way he carries out his job. Jaggers' responses to Pip's questions about his benefactor cause Pip to draw some foolish conclusions. What are they?

159/162	Pip
148/181	Jaggers
158/164	Expectations

161 'Choose your bridge, . . .'
The total separation of public life and private feeling is once again illustrated in Wemmick's humorous response to Pip's question.

107/162	Wemmick

Chapter 37

162 Deeming Sunday the . . .
Wemmick's home and caring life-style remind the reader of Pip's rejection of Joe's love. The Aged Parent's remark, 'His business is law', makes an appropriate comment on civil and criminal law. It has little to do with justice, or the rights or wrongs of a case, but everything to do with business and making money.

160/164	Pip
161/163	Wemmick

163 As Wemmick and . . .
The humorous account of Wemmick courting Miss Skiffins enhances the atmosphere of warmth and caring affection in the castle. It also provides a contrast to the unsatisfactory and cold love affair that Pip tries to carry on with Estella, with a marked lack of success.

162/164	Wemmick
156/165	Relationships

164 Before a week was out, . . .
Pip arranges, through Wemmick, a place in a business for Herbert; this will have useful consequences later in the novel. For so long the recipient of others' anonymous gifts, Pip now becomes an anonymous benefactor himself. It is perhaps the first real act of generosity he has indulged in, though ironically, it is with someone else's money.

162/165	Pip
151/182	Herbert
163/203	Wemmick
160/169	Expectations

Chapter 38

165 I saw her often . . .
Pip often escorts Estella during her time in Richmond. However, note the total waste of time it is in terms of furthering his cause with her: 'I never had one hour's happiness . . .'. Do Estella's warnings to him suggest a growing affection for Pip, or are they more a warning that she cannot be responsible for actions which might eventually cause him serious disappointment?

164/168	Pip
149/166	Estella
163/166	Relationships

166 She was even more . . .
From the beginning of this paragraph with its repetition of the image-laden word 'hung' to the end of the fourth paragraph on '. . . beetles on the floor', the 'darkened and unhealthy house' and its equally unhealthy owner are once again displayed in all their compelling distortion. Is there any evidence here that Pip is beginning to recognize Miss Havisham's perverted intentions with regard to himself and Estella, and that her expectations for him are anything but 'great'?

165/167	Estella
156/167	Miss Havisham
165/167	Relationships

167 We were seated . . .
The exchange between Estella and Miss Havisham comes as a considerable surprise to the reader. Nowhere is there any indication given that such a dispute might arise. However, note how perfectly Miss Havisham has been caught in her own trap. By teaching Estella to be hard and have no feelings, she has by the same token excluded herself from any chance of being loved by Estella, and suddenly, she seems to desire that very thing. Notice the formal, theatrical quality of the dialogue, the rhetorical questions – 'Did I never . . .', the repetition of emotive words – 'So proud . . . , so hard . . .'; yet it is surely not possible that either Miss Havisham or Estella is playing a part. What is indicated here about the two women, and what role has Estella been brought up to play?

166/174	Estella
166/176	Miss Havisham
166/198	Relationships

168 'Estella who?' said I.
Note this rather juvenile conversation between Pip and Drummle. Do you think it shows either of them in a very good light? In Pip's final conversation with Estella in this section of the novel she makes her intentions quite clear to Pip: he would not appear to be included in her plans.

165/169	Pip
111/194	Drummle

169 In the Eastern story, . . .
The short story which Pip recounts prepares us for the traumas to come. Perhaps we should not be too surprised that Pip's world is about to collapse, given his recent conversation with Estella!

168/171	Pip
164/173	Expectations

Chapter 39

170 I was three-and-twenty . . .
We are given a brief statement of the facts and changes in Pip's life at the beginning of this chapter. Why do you think the author felt it necessary to do this?

157/178	Structure

171 It was wretched weather; . . .
Note how the atmosphere and weather of London replicates that of the marshes some years ago when Pip met the convict. In particular you will probably remember how the river and sea were then seen as threatening images.

169/172	Pip
159/224	Atmosphere
150/195	Imagery

172 I had asked him . . .
The convict Magwitch, rather unrealistically, expects instant recognition. Pip does eventually recognize him, and launches into a very condescending little speech – '"Stay!" said I . . .', which is very formal and full of high moral tone.

171/173	Pip
56/173	Magwitch

173 'May I make so bold,' . . .
At last Pip learns the true source of his expectations and, to say the least, the news is not welcome. All his snobbish values and false sentiment are thrown into the dust where they belong. When Magwitch finally claims recognition for having made Pip a 'gentleman', Pip can only shrink in fear and dread as from a 'terrible beast'.

172/174	Pip
172/174	Magwitch
169/177	Expectations

174 O Estella, Estella!
Pip has yet to learn how ironic is his concern about Estella!

173/177	Pip
167/190	Estella
173/175	Magwitch

175 O, that he had never come!
Pip may well bemoan his fate, and maybe he would have been better off at the forge. Nevertheless, though Magwitch might have started badly in his quest to turn Pip into a gentleman, his return to England will at last cause the desired effect, though at great cost to himself. Certainly, we now see the convict in a new light; all the mysteries of Pip's expectations have been explained, and we know Magwitch to be a man of his word, fulfilling the promise of that thoughtful look he gave Pip so long ago as he was taken away to resume his captivity.

174/176	Magwitch

176 'And then, dear boy, . . .'
Be aware of the parallel between Magwitch and Miss Havisham. Do they both use and shape the life of a child into adulthood in order to take revenge on society? Do they have any other motives?

175/177	Magwitch
167/189	Miss Havisham

177 Nothing was needed . . .
Pip shows the first small sign of redeeming himself. The next nine paragraphs of this chapter act almost as a review of Pip's life so far, his hopes and expectations. They illustrate that he is now miserably aware of how he has been used and abused by Miss Havisham, and how his grandiose expectations are as nothing.

174/179	Pip
176/180	Magwitch
173/180	Expectations

Chapter 40

178 'I judged the person . . .'
No sooner has Magwitch returned than Pip is plunged into yet more mysteries. Who was the stranger on the stairs and why was he there?

170/182	Structure

179 All this time . . .
How long is it since Pip thought of anyone else before himself? Even when he thought of Estella, it was self-centred in that it concentrated on the pain he was suffering because she rejected his love.

177/180   Pip

180 He took out of . . .
Pip shows a marked lack of interest in the appearance of his 'great expectations'. This seems to be because of his growing concern for the safety of Magwitch. Suddenly, the centre of Pip's world is no longer Pip!

179/181   Pip
177/182   Magwitch
177/183   Expectations

181 'Now, Pip,' said he, . . .
Jaggers immediately recognizes from Pip's face and manner that something exceptional has happened. Note how he protects himself through recognizing only the letter of the law and refusing to be told anything that he might have to react to on an official level. Notice the devious 'double-talk' about 'Provis'.

180/183   Pip
160/210   Jaggers

182 'Do so, as he . . .'
Magwitch makes Herbert take an oath of secrecy. There is a parallel here with an event long ago when he first met Pip.

180/183   Magwitch
164/185   Herbert
178/190   Structure

Chapter 41

183 In vain should I . . .
From now on, everything Magwitch says and does undermines Pip's social pretensions, and in doing so it gradually releases Pip from the trap of false gentility. From this stage on see whether or not Pip's better instincts start operating more freely.

181/184   Pip
182/186   Magwitch
180/184   Expectations

184 'Then' said I, . . .
Having decided that he can accept no more money from Magwitch, Pip, in this brief paragraph, recognizes the depths to which he has sunk: 'heavily in debt', 'no expectations', 'bred to no calling', 'fit for nothing'. The accuracy of his analysis cannot be doubted, but the very accuracy points at the fact that Pip is starting to emerge as a better person, and one who will be capable of rectifying this situation.

183/185   Pip
183/185   Expectations

185 Poor fellow! He little . . .
Herbert's offer to Pip of the chance to earn a living in the company where he expects a partnership is deeply ironic. As yet, Pip has not thought of the consequences for Herbert of his decision to reject Magwitch's money. It will be interesting to see how he resolves it.

184/186   Pip
182/186   Herbert
184/198   Expectations

186 'And you have, and are . . .'
What was the previous occasion when Herbert so accurately and effectively analysed Pip's feelings for, and reaction to, someone? It throws some light onto Herbert's character that he can make such clear assessments. It is here that Pip fully acknowledges his own life comes second to his concern for Magwitch and it marks an important stage in his growing maturity.

Chapter 42

187 'Dear boy and Pip's . . .'
The story of Magwitch's childhood reflects one of Dickens's major themes in all his works – that of abandoned, orphaned, or maltreated children. How many of them have we met so far in this novel?

188 'At Epsom races, . . .'
The relevance of this detailed story about Compeyson is not immediately obvious but will become so. Meanwhile, he serves as yet another illustration of a 'gentleman'.

189 'There was another . . .'
The gaps in the reader's knowledge of Miss Havisham's story are being filled in, as the reader will soon realize. Note the complicated picture which is building up!

190 He looked about him . . .
Magwitch's mysterious reference to a wife is significant in setting the scene for exposing Estella's origins.

191 'When we was . . .'
There are two matters aired in the description of the trial: one is the lack of real justice in the courts, and the other is the false value which society gives to a man's appearance.

192 'By my boy, I . . .'
The mystery of the other convict whom Magwitch pursued through the marsh is cleared up. But we are left not knowing his fate. The disclosure, moments later, of his relationship with Miss Havisham must make the reader certain that he will yet make an appearance.

Chapter 43

193 Next day, I had . . .
The comment of Pip's about the meanness he was capable of towards 'Joe or his name', suggests that Pip still has some way to go before he has completely redeemed himself.

		Characters and ideas previous/next comment
185/193	Pip	
183/187	Magwitch	
185/203	Herbert	
186/189	Magwitch	
154/191	Social aspects	
0/189	Compeyson	
187/190	Magwitch	
176/197	Miss Havisham	
188/191	Compeyson	
174/195	Estella	
189/192	Magwitch	
182/201	Structure	
189/192	Compeyson	
187/220	Social aspects	
191/202	Compeyson	
190/202	Magwitch	
186/194	Pip	

194 As he pretended . . .
It is some while since we have seen Drummle. This incident serves to refresh our minds as to his character but also restates the love that Pip still has for Estella. It is also a comic satire on the 'gentlemanly' and ridiculous dispute they have over access to the warmth of the fire. The reference in the second to last paragraph of the chapter to Drummle's 'blundering brutal manner' with the horse will find its echo when we hear the circumstances of his death, later in the story. At the end of the chapter the shadowy figure of Orlick re-emerges to give the reader something else to think about.

193/196	Pip
168/210	Drummle
157/222	Orlick

Chapter 44

195 In the room . . .
Estella's knitting, and her hands, will be an important linking image for Pip – with regard to what?

190/199	Estella
171/204	Imagery

196 'Miss Havisham,' said I, . . .
We see a more assured Pip here. Note how he neatly turns Miss Havisham's dismissive image 'what wind blows you here' to his own advantage.

194/197	Pip

197 'I was liberally paid . . .'
The immediate purpose of Pip's visit is disclosed; it is not to request something for himself but for his friend Herbert, and, in promoting Herbert's cause, Pip shows a degree of moral growth in his character. How does Miss Havisham react to this approach? Does her reaction suggest anything about a change in her character?

196/198	Pip
189/198	Miss Havisham

198 I saw Miss Havisham . . .
How well do you think that Pip's point in the previous paragraph struck home with Miss Havisham? Estella, however, is as unmoved as ever and despite Pip's quite dignified words she shows no emotion when telling him she is to marry Drummle. Compare her calmness with Miss Havisham's reaction.

197/199	Pip
197/213	Miss Havisham
185/199	Expectations
167/199	Relationships

199 'On whom should I . . .'
That Miss Havisham wanted Estella to delay her marriage to Drummle comes as something of a surprise. Was there any previous suggestion of a change of heart on her part? Or can you think of any other reason why she should suggest a delay?

198/200	Pip
195/200	Estella
198/200	Expectations
198/200	Relationships

200 'Out of my thoughts!'
Pip's impassioned parting speech to Estella leaves us with the knowledge that Pip now recognizes that his love was based on illusion. In what way does he realize that his love is based on self-delusion and imagination?

199/202	Pip
199/205	Estella
199/207	Expectations
199/205	Relationships

Characters and ideas previous/next comment

201 Much surprised by . . .
After such a traumatic chapter, Pip is met by this mysterious and worrying note. It reintroduces the problems of Magwitch and turns the reader's attention away from the saga of Estella and Miss Havisham which, for the moment at least, seems complete.

190/209   Structure

Chapter 45

202 'I accidentally heard, . . .'
After a sleepless night, appropriately in a vault-like room, worrying about the cryptic note, Pip now has his worst fears confirmed. Compeyson is back, and obviously in pursuit of Magwitch.

200/205   Pip
192/204   Magwitch
192/230   Compeyson

203 'Mr Herbert,' said Wemmick, . . .
Both Wemmick and Herbert have played a very active part in aiding Pip and Magwitch, and in doing so they demonstrate qualities which are to be admired. Would you agree they are both 'gentleman'? Can you yet define what makes a 'gentleman'?

186/207   Herbert
164/204   Wemmick

204 'The house with the . . .'
News of where Herbert has found Magwitch a hiding place reintroduces the importance of the river in the story. It was the river that brought Magwitch, and it will provide the route for his attempted escape.

202/217   Magwitch
203/220   Wemmick
195/207   Imagery

Chapter 46

205 As we were thus . . .
What do you notice about Pip's reaction to meeting Herbert's young lady, Clara? Is there evidence that Pip is developing a realistic set of values? Note his comment near the end of this chapter when he refers to 'the redeeming youth and trust and hope' which marks Herbert's and Clara's relationship. There was never any such feeling between himself and Estella.

202/206   Pip
200/210   Estella
200/234   Relationships

206 Herbert, who had been . . .
Pip's ability to row will now be put to something more useful than it was previously. How does this indicate the further change in Pip's character and life-style?

205/207   Pip

207 In short, I was . . .
Note the difference between Herbert's and Pip's view of the river: it is totally conditioned by the fortune it represents for them. For Pip and Magwitch it represents destroyed expectations but for Herbert and his future with Clara it reflects 'great expectations'.

206/208   Pip
203/221   Herbert
200/208   Expectations
204/211   Imagery

Chapter 47

	Characters and ideas	
	previous/next comment	

208 My worldly affairs . . .

By struggling to cope with his debts and not asking Magwitch for money, Pip shows a greater readiness to come to terms with the realities of the world, and in doing so strengthens his own character.

| 207/209 | Pip |
| 207/212 | Expectations |

209 As it was a raw . . .

Wopsle's theatrical decline parallels in somewhat more comic form the loss of Pip's expectations. The comedy provided by Wopsle helps relieve moments of dramatic tension, but, some paragraphs on, he also brings Pip back to the reality of his situation when he tells Pip he recognized Compeyson sitting behind him in the theatre.

208/211	Pip
140/0	Wopsle
201/217	Structure

Chapter 48

210 We went to Gerrard-street, . . .

The news that Miss Havisham wants to see Pip makes the reader wonder why. However, the comments of Wemmick and Jaggers about the 'question of supremacy' between Estella and Drummle prepare us for the later news of how she is treated by him.

205/211	Estella
181/219	Jaggers
194/0	Drummle

211 The action of her . . .

At last, Pip makes the connection between Estella and Molly. The central importance of the hand image for Pip is now seen as it brings the final confirmation of the illusory nature of Pip's expectations and dreams with regard to Estella.

209/212	Pip
210/212	Estella
110/212	Molly
207/214	Imagery

212 'A score or so . . .'

This account of Molly's trial adds another large fragment to the detailed picture of those whose lives have touched on Pip's expectations. Note how Estella is now shown *not* to have come from the ranks of society. Does Pip still love her?

208/218	Pip
211/217	Estella
211/219	Molly
208/218	Expectations

Chapter 49

213 Doing as I had . . .

Both Miss Havisham and Pip have changed and their conversation provides us with a view of two characters who are very different from those we knew in earlier parts of the story. Over the next few pages we see in great detail how Miss Havisham bitterly regrets and grieves for her actions with regard to Pip and Estella. Pip learns all she has to tell about Estella, but still not who her father was. We have seen changes in Miss Havisham; what view is presented here of Pip?

| 212/214 | Pip |
| 198/214 | Miss Havisham |

214 Taking the brewery . . .

Yet again we have a repetition of the 'hanging image' in the brewery. But this time it gives Pip a warning presentiment which causes him to go and check Miss Havisham. In endeavouring to put out the flames, Pip destroys the

213/215	Pip
213/216	Miss Havisham
211/215	Imagery

mouldering heap that was the wedding feast, and she is eventually placed on her bed which had been carried into the room and put on the great table. Can you remember the prophecy that Miss Havisham made about the table on one of Pip's visits to Satis House? Can the burning wedding dress be seen as a symbol of Miss Havisham's destruction by her own obsession?

215 She was insensible, . . .
Consider whether the burning of Pip's hands symbolizes the end of the imagery associated with hands, and perhaps a symbolic destruction of all his old ways and false aspirations.

214/218	Pip
214/224	Imagery

216 There was a stage, . . .
Does the repetition of those three key phrases suggest the state of Miss Havisham's mind, and her recognition of the wrong she has done? Note in the next paragraph the fine action of Pip in kissing the woman who has done so much to blight his life.

214/240	Miss Havisham

Chapter 50

217 'So you did. And so . . .'
The final piece of the puzzle which has so exercised Pip's, and the readers', minds is now revealed: Magwitch is Estella's father. The hold that Compeyson had over Magwitch is also explained. Be aware of how carefully the whole jigsaw has been constructed now that all the complicated interlinking parts have been revealed to us. It only remains to see how the final act will be played and how all the other loose ends will be resolved. Can you list the events which have now to run their course and the characters whose fates we need to know?

212/219	Estella
204/222	Magwitch
212/0	Molly
209/220	Structure

Chapter 51

218 But I could not . . .
If this meeting is compared with those earlier ones which Pip had with Jaggers, it is impressive to see the self-assuredness which he now displays. He outlines his findings with a calmness and confidence which has Jaggers listening to every word: a no mean feat! Jaggers' attempt here to regain control of the situation is swept away by Pip's appeal for frankness and manliness.

215/219	Pip
212/221	Expectations

219 'Pip,' said Mr Jaggers, . . .
The revelation of Wemmick's private side has the extraordinary effect of bringing an actual smile to Jaggers' face. Closely following this glimpse of humanity, Jaggers reveals that behind that cold, calculating lawyer's front, there is actually a compassionate human being who once attempted to rescue a little child: Jaggers' humanity was perhaps the best-kept secret of the book! His revelations about his actions regarding Estella serve to confirm the detail of what Pip already knew.

218/221	Pip
217/247	Estella
210/220	Jaggers

220 Standing by for a little, . . .
The revelation of a human side in each of these men causes a momentary problem in their working relationship. It is a moment which they both soon find opportunity to eradicate by rounding on the unfortunate Mike and condemning his 'feelings' with some ferocity. The demands of their unhappy profession allow no such luxury! Can you remember the last occasion we met Mike and the treatment he got from Wemmick?

Chapter 52

221 From Little Britain, I . . .
Pip's pleasure in completing the arrangements for Herbert's partnership illustrates the extent to which he has redeemed himself from his self-centred way of life.

222 'If you are not . . .'
A further mysterious element is introduced by this note. Coming so soon after Wemmick's note that indicated the time to move Magwitch had arrived, this latest note is far more compelling in its implied threat to the success of Pip's venture. His decision to go without discussing the matter with anyone is perhaps foolhardy, but in keeping with this new Pip who is so unthinking of himself, and so concerned for the well-being of his friends. (But does this concern embrace Joe yet?)

223 I thought, 'Yet Joe, . . .'
The claims of the impostor Pumblechook serve their purpose of bringing Joe forcefully back into Pip's mind. He recognizes here just how much he owes to Joe and Biddy. Pip's heart is 'deeply and most deservedly humbled'.

Chapter 53

224 It was a dark night, . . .
The return to the marshes with its wind and loneliness reminds us of Pip's first visit when he was threatened by the convict.

225 His enjoyment of . . .
Orlick's attempt to murder Pip further complicates the plot. However, in some ways it does seem to fulfil the promise of those threatening moments on the marsh when we first met the young Pip. Note the concerns which cause Pip unhappiness if he should be killed – his friends would think he had deserted them; he has not a thought for himself. This surely is a very different Pip from the one we used to know.

226 'It was you, villain,' . . .
This meeting with Orlick allows a few more loose ends to be tied. Orlick is confirmed as the one who attacked Mrs Joe, as the person on the stairs of Pip's lodgings, and as a watcher in the shadows whilst Pip tried to protect Magwitch by disguising him, hiding him and calling him uncle. The fortuitous loss of Orlick's note leads Pip's friends to him, together with Pip's old tormentor, Trabb's boy, who turns out to be not so bad after all and who is rewarded by a grateful Pip.

225/227	Pip
225/241	Orlick
136/0	Trabb's boy
225/227	Structure

227 Wednesday morning was . . .
Note how for the very first time in the novel Pip seems to view the marshes with a confidence totally lacking in any fear of the place. Indeed the whole atmosphere is lighter and 'a veil seemed to be drawn'.

226/228	Pip
224/229	Imagery
226/243	Structure

Chapter 54

228 It was one of . . .
Read the opening of this important chapter carefully. In what ways does the reader know that Pip is a totally changed character?

227/229	Pip
222/229	Magwitch
223/231	Expectations

229 He dipped his hand . . .
The combination of the imagery implied in both the river and the constant reference to hands gains a new significance. The inevitability of the turn of the tide, the hands that can grasp at the water but not hold it, the promise and the threat that they represent in the lives of the characters who people the novel all seem to be contained in these two images.

228/231	Pip
228/230	Magwitch
227/230	Imagery

230 At the same moment, . . .
The river that brought the two convicts into Pip's life is now the scene of their final meeting. The fight between the convicts, again in the river, exactly replicates their first conflict and brings the novel full circle for them. In drowning Compeyson, Magwitch sustains wounds which will prove fatal and thus enable him to cheat the hangman's rope.

229/231	Magwitch
202/0	Compeyson
229/232	Imagery

231 When I asked this . . .
Pip's expectations are lost – confiscated by the Crown. Why does Pip want Magwitch to retain his illusion that Pip will inherit the wealth for which Magwitch had worked so hard?

229/232	Pip
230/232	Magwitch
228/238	Expectations

232 For now, my repugnance . . .
The symbolic promise of the river is realized. Its destructive force upon Magwitch also liberates and cleanses, and leaves him and Pip free to be transformed and redeemed by love. Here we see Pip with all pretension stripped away, free to find his own standards of what is right and of true value.

231/233	Pip
231/237	Magwitch
230/246	Imagery

Characters and ideas previous/next comment

Chapter 55

233 He was taken . . .
Jaggers demonstrates his practical, professional self to the full. How do his feelings about Magwitch's money and forthcoming trial show his realism?

232/234	Pip
220/0	Jaggers

234 It was at this . . .
Notice the open, loving relationship between Pip and Herbert. Perhaps the best thing Pip gained directly through his expectations was the lasting friendship of Herbert.

233/236	Pip
221/0	Herbert
205/236	Relationships

235 'Thank you, thank you . . .'
Wemmick regrets the 'sacrifice of so much portable property'. The invitation to Pip to join him in a walk does nothing to prepare us for what is to come! His marriage to Miss Skiffins is very humorously portrayed, as he acquires his most precious of 'portable properties'.

220/0	Wemmick

236 Wemmick came down . . .
Both of Pip's true companions, Herbert and Wemmick, are now married. Pip is alone, far from Biddy and Joe, and Estella, who is also married. Pip's isolation is complete.

234/238	Pip
234/238	Relationships

Chapter 56

237 The trial was . . .
Read the trial scene carefully – these next five paragraphs give a chilling picture of 'justice' at work. Thirty-two men and women in the dock, together receive the sentence of death. There is no individual consideration, no humanity, certainly no real evidence of justice. Yet note the dignity of Magwitch. You would do well here to call to mind both the 'bundle of shivers' and the monster that came out of the 'distant savage lair'; do we see either of them now?

232/238	Magwitch
220/0	Social aspects

238 The number of days . . .
Magwitch's money had at first been the cause of Pip's failure to become a gentleman; now, in having effectively rejected it, Pip has been freed to become a true gentleman. Magwitch at last has his wish for Pip realized. The convict's last hours are a fine moment for both these characters, and Pip's revelation to Magwitch that his daughter is alive and loved by Pip is a fitting climax to their relationship.

236/239	Pip
237/0	Magwitch
231/239	Expectations
236/239	Relationships

Chapter 57

239 After I had turned . . .
Pip's illness brings Joe back into his life and his love for Joe becomes apparent. Note his cry a paragraph or so on, 'O Joe, you break my heart!' It is Joe's love which 'breaks' Pip, not his infatuation for Estella. Further on in

238/242	Pip
238/240	Expectations
238/0	Relationships

Characters and ideas previous/next comment

this conversation he gives voice to his realization of what Joe really is, a 'gentle Christian man'. At last, Joe's character is fully revealed and appreciated by Pip.

240 'Is she dead Joe?'
The death of Miss Havisham and the details of her will, with the righting of the wrongs done to Matthew Pocket and with the other Pockets getting their just desserts, neatly ties up a number of loose ends about which the reader wants to know.

216/0	Miss Havisham
100/0	Matthew
239/242	Expectations

241 The accuracy of these . . .
Orlick's arrest for housebreaking, and the humiliation of Pumblechook whose house he broke into, neatly bring their part in the story to an end. You might wonder, though, if Orlick was sufficiently punished for murdering Mrs Joe and attempting to murder Pip!

226/0	Orlick
223/243	Pumblechook

242 The purpose was, . . .
Pip's remaining illusion, that his creditor had withdrawn, is shattered when he learns that Joe has paid off his debts. His last expectation, that Biddy will be prepared to marry him, will shortly be put to the test.

239/244	Pip
223/244	Biddy
240/245	Expectations

Chapter 58

243 Early in the morning . . .
Satis House, which had been the scene of so many painful moments for Pip, is to be pulled down. A few paragraphs on, Pumblechook makes a last appearance, showing that he has changed not one bit from the moment we first met him.

241/0	Pumblechook
224/0	Atmosphere
227/247	Structure

244 'It's my wedding day,' . . .
Pip's final expectation is demolished, but in the process Joe is rewarded with a bright future in the company of Biddy, and ironically, Pip is left free eventually to be with Estella.

242/245	Pip
223/0	Joe
242/246	Biddy

245 Many a year went round, . . .
Pip's life is at last successful, not as a result of great expectations but because of hard work and friendship.

244/246	Pip
242/0	Expectations

Chapter 59

246 Biddy looked down at . . .
Eleven years later Pip has returned to the forge – now the home it could have been in his childhood. Notice how one might say Biddy is bringing young Pip up 'by hand', but the image represents a real home with parents who love him; it is the sort of home which was denied to those many orphans who featured so largely in the story.

245/247	Pip
244/0	Biddy
232/247	Imagery

247 A cold silvery mist . . .
Note how the image of stars shining beyond the mist brings to mind Estella.
With Pip's return to the garden of Satis House all the old painful memories
are laid to rest, as if they were demolished along with the house. It is a fitting
moment for Estella to join him and repeat the walk they took there so many
years ago. At the end, the mists which had obscured much of Pip's vision of
life are lifting and his future with Estella is assured.

Characters and ideas
previous/next comment

246/0   Pip
219/0   Estella
246/0   Imagery
243/0   Structure

Characters
in the novel

This is a very brief overview of each character. You should use it as a starting point for your own studies of characterization. For each of the aspects of character mentioned you should look in your text for evidence to support or contradict the views expressed here, and indeed, your own views as well.

Know the incidents and conversations which will support and enlarge upon your knowledge of each character. You will find it helpful to select a character and follow the commentary, referring always to the text to read and digest the context of the comment.

Biddy

Biddy represents the reality of woman in contrast to Pip's romantic view of Estella. Pip uses her as a confidante because she is wise, patient and warm. She is also truthful and realistic and prepared to reproach Pip for his sometimes thoughtless words and actions (see chapters 17, 19 and 35). Notice his most ungentlemanly conduct in response to her comments. As you read the novel look for evidence of her feelings for Pip – feelings of which he seems totally unaware.

Biddy puts into words the moral values that Joe holds but cannot successfully articulate. She is also an orphan, but unlike many of the other orphans she would not appear to have any expectations. Consider how she helps Pip and then Joe to read; with the latter the teaching is not done with any attempt to make Joe better or different but to give him the enjoyment that the ability to read would bring.

Compeyson

Compeyson is the man who jilted Miss Havisham on her wedding day after embezzling large amounts of her money. He was responsible for leading Magwitch into major crime, but because of his gentlemanly appearance and plausible tongue he managed to get a lesser sentence than Magwitch when they were both caught.

He appears very briefly in the novel (chapters 3, 5 and 47) but his presence is felt through both Magwitch's and Miss Havisham's stories. Representing largely unmotivated evil in his dealings with others, he is presented to us as yet another 'gentleman' against whom to measure Pip's aspirations.

Bentley Drummle

Bentley Drummle is one of the examples put to us of a 'gentleman'. His expectation is of a baronet's title to which only an accident of birth entitles him; he certainly does not merit it or otherwise earn the respect which would surely be associated with it. His heavy appearance and his sullen and arrogant manner place him in sharp contrast with both Herbert and Pip. He is a clear reminder that money and class do not automatically make a gentleman.

If Estella had married Pip before marrying Drummle do you think Pip would have been able to overcome the prejudices which Miss Havisham had impressed upon her? Did it need Drummle to make her suffer (as Miss Havisham had hoped Estella would make men suffer) and return her to a normal human perspective on life – one where she would more easily respond to Pip's love? Certainly, she was unable to break Drummle's spirit and so fulfil Miss Havisham's plan to take her revenge on men. Only a fatal accident on a horse he had mistreated was able to destroy his brutish life.

Estella

Estella – Miss Havisham's adopted daughter – is used by her as a means of taking revenge on men. She is brought up to have a cold indifference to all human feelings and the attentions of the opposite sex. Her name comes from the Latin for a star, and, like a star, she remains cold and distant despite all Pip's attempts to get close to her. Both she and Pip see themselves as destined for each other by Miss Havisham; they both certainly spring to do her every bidding. Is there a spark of humanity in Estella? If not, why does she keep warning Pip against falling in love with her?

The effect of Estella's upbringing backfires on Miss Havisham, as Estella can love no one. Her dispute with Miss Havisham in chapter 38 is one of which you should take careful note as it tells us much about the two women. It is implied that her experiences during marriage to the cruel Drummle have softened her, but do you perhaps feel that this redemption, so undeveloped in the narrative, remains unconvincing?

Joe Gargery

Joe, the good-natured countryman, the village blacksmith, is a character who is gradually revealed to the reader. At first he appears kindly but weak (witness his relationships with Mrs Joe, Pumblechook and Miss Havisham). However, his responses to events throughout the novel show true humanity, strength, intelligent tact and an inner pride and sense of purpose, combined with a total contentment with his place in the social order.

That said, one can imagine how frustrating and embarrassing Pip will have found some of his ways and mannerisms as he grows up. Joe provides comic moments with his struggle to express himself, but, whilst the reader may sometimes find him annoying, we never see Joe as an object of pity – he is too self-contained to inspire that reaction. At the end of the novel Joe emerges as a figure whom Pip fully respects. He also serves as a prime example of the fact that social status and money have nothing whatsoever to do with being a gentleman.

Miss Havisham

Fantastic and eccentric, Miss Havisham presides in isolation over her macabre house. The images of decay and death which surround her give the clues to the effects she has on both Pip and Estella. Estella is imbued with an attitude towards men that will cause her great unhappiness, and Pip's belief that Miss Havisham is responsible for his expectations is cruelly fired by her. She does her best to ruin both lives before she finally realizes the enormity of the selfishness of her actions.

She no longer lives in the real world; the stopped clocks, the wedding feast still on the table, and the clothes she wears all bear witness to this. Her melodramatic death is appropriate to the life she led. Her whole life has been composed of behavioural extremes, thus her repentance is convincing because it represents yet another extreme of behaviour. She becomes as obsessed with the desire to be forgiven as she once was with the desire to avenge herself on all men through Estella. Her money brought her nothing but unhappiness, greedy relatives, and power; but even the power it gave her over Pip and Estella, eventually came to nothing.

Mr and Mrs Hubble

These are examples of the way Dickens achieves lively characterization in even the lesser characters. The Hubbles play an essential part in Mrs Joe's circle of friends, encouraging Mrs Joe in her attitudes and actions with regard to Pip, and thereby enabling the author to give Mrs Joe much more depth in his portrayal of her.

Jaggers

Jaggers is the overbearing but respected lawyer who, for much of the novel, is the key figure in all the mystery surrounding Pip. His determination to keep what he knows to himself, neither to confirm nor deny anything, is essential to the success of the story. He knew the secret of Estella's mother and administered Miss Havisham's desires in respect of Estella. He was Magwitch's agent in the fulfilling of his plans for Pip. Thus he provides a link between all parties. Did he know that Estella was Magwitch's daughter?

His office embodies the spirit of the Victorian legal system, particularly in the symbolism of the death-masks of two of his executed clients, and in the seemingly cold and callous way in which he carries out his professional responsibilities. Jaggers dominates his part of London, called Little Britain, but why is he always washing his hands of all he comes into contact with?

He is one of Dickens's more fully developed characters but, interestingly, he is not fully revealed. The reader never really knows Jaggers and the one suggestion that he once knew how to dream is never explained.

Mrs Joe

Aggressive, unmaternal and unwifely, Mrs Joe glories in martyrdom whilst displaying social pretensions. She is responsible for much of Pip's insecurity and guilt. Tickler and a vicious tongue are her instruments of punishment. As you read the story you might consider whether Joe feels that she has any redeeming features – if there are any, he should be able to point us to them.

Her lingering death after a violent attack by Orlick ensures that Biddy comes into close contact with Joe and helps move the plot on in respect of their relationship. Does Mrs Joe's long illness create any sympathetic response in the reader? Can you see that to an extent she parallels Miss Havisham in her influence on Pip? In her illness and death does she also, like Miss Havisham, ask forgiveness of the people she has wronged: Orlick, Joe and Pip? Was there something in her life that turned her against men? Has she had a great expectation thwarted? There is no obvious evidence for such a theory in the story, but such parallels as there are with Miss Havisham make one wonder.

Magwitch

Also known as Provis and Mr Campbell, the convict Magwitch is another of the story's orphans. At the beginning he is an object of terror for Pip, but his decision, when captured, to take the blame for the theft of the pie and file shows some feeling for Pip. By the time he has returned to see 'his gentleman' he has become the key to the mysteries that surround Pip's wealth and the parents of Estella. At the final stage of the novel, he turns from being an object of revulsion to Pip into a person whom Pip pities and respects.

When we know more of his origins we can have some sympathy for Magwitch, but he is no passive victim of society as may be seen when he seeks revenge against Compeyson and eventually kills him. By the time of his trial and death he has a certain dignity which did not seem to be evident when he was the animal which 'glared and growled' and frightened Pip half to death at the beginning of the novel. As a test for Pip's maturity and real love, his return at the end of the book shows just how much Pip has grown from a small 'bundle of shivers' into a mature man.

Molly

With strong hands and a scarred wrist, Jaggers' housekeeper, Molly, is described as a 'wild beast tamed'. Once tried for murder she is an unlikely mother for the beautiful, passionless Estella, but she provides a key to unravelling the mystery for Pip. Her very presence at Jaggers' also says something about the man behind the mask which he adopts in front of his clients and acquaintances.

Orlick

It is worth comparing Orlick with Drummle. Both are physically large and loutish and though Orlick does not aspire to be a gentleman he does show some considerable interest in Biddy. He was no real threat to Pip's ambitions here, such as they were, but then, did Pip give to Biddy the same intensity of emotion that he gave to Estella, where Drummle was a very real threat?

Orlick shows some sharpness in his arguing for a half-day holiday when Pip was allowed time off from the forge, and in his summing up of Mrs Joe's character. But his insolence, brutishness and savagery, especially in his attacks on Mrs Joe and Pip, are the moments for which we remember him most.

Pip

Of all the characters in the novel, Pip is the one who develops most. You must be able to identify the stages in his transition from a 'small bundle of shivers' to a mature business man with a strong sense of loyalty, right and honesty. His role as narrator of the story is of fundamental importance to the way we learn about him and his companions.

As a child he is intelligent, imaginative and eager for knowledge but he is also sensitive, timid and guilt-ridden. His contacts with Miss Havisham and Estella, and his 'great expectations', create aspirations which lead to snobbery and false moral values which outweigh his finer instincts. It is because he is, in a sense, a victim of immaturity, coincidence and romantic illusion that he retains the sympathy of the reader. When the foundation of his snobbery is destroyed he begins to move towards a moral strength which has respect and love for his fellow man, regardless of social standing and prestige, as its core.

At the novel's end the mature Pip, though a redeemed character, seems to be a man saddened by a learning experience, and displaying only a modest optimism about the future.

Herbert Pocket

Herbert represents the combination of the social and moral qualities of a true gentleman. He is honest yet tactful, socially aware but not a snob, and, most important, a true and loyal friend to Pip. His success in business is created by 'cheerful industry'.

Matthew Pocket

A promising scholar, but without financial resources, Matthew Pocket, as a man of integrity, demonstrates an independence of spirit and a determination to be 'his own man', which Pip could do worse than copy. He provides another link in the mysteries surrounding Pip by being a distant relative of Miss Havisham, but out of favour with her for warning her about Compeyson. Married to a lady of high birth, he has never lived up to his wife's expectations of him, but he does not seem any the worse for it. Conversely, Pip only narrowly escapes his moral destruction when he follows the path of expectations provided by other people. Pip's intervention leads to Matthew's being provided for in Miss Havisham's will.

Mrs Pocket and the Pockets

Daughter of a family with claim to a title, mother to a large chaotic family, and quite useless as the female head of the household, Dickens describes Mrs Pocket with humour whilst displaying dislike of false gentility and upper class snobbery.

Sarah, whose envious nature shows on her face, which changes 'from brown to green and yellow' when she sees Pip dressed up after his 'expectations' have been announced, is fearful of others who might benefit from Miss Havisham's money. She finally goes to work for her at Satis House but only gains a small amount in the will. Camilla only pretends affection and fellow feeling for Miss Havisham. Georgina, who is married, is a greedy, miserable woman who does likewise.

Miss Havisham's dislike of these relatives leads her to allow them and Pip to believe she is responsible for Pip's 'expectations'. As a group they represent that large body of people who do little or nothing to justify their existence and act like parasites on those with more money. They also provide a means of showing that Miss Havisham's anger at men had spilled over onto all humanity, and that she had totally lost any perspective in her dealings with fellow human beings.

Pumblechook

In describing Pumblechook as a 'fearful impostor', Pip lays him bare for the hypocrite he undoubtedly is. However, he also presents another proof to us of the fact that wealth does not make a gentleman. His 'adoption' of Joe's family circle, as though he were the head of the household, his cruelty to Pip at the early stages of the story, his obsequiousness when Pip comes into great expectations and his rudeness at the end when Pip's fortunes decline, present a clear picture of anything but gentlemanly behaviour.

He represents the kind of cruelty young Pip suffers from the adult world and the greed and hidden aggression connected with pretentiousness and lack of humanity.

Trabb's boy

Trabb's boy is a character who pops up at various points in the narrative. Pip fears his caustic tongue and lack of 'respect' for his own new-found status as a person of expectations. He is present when Pip is transformed by his master from a blacksmith's boy into a 'gentleman' by the simple addition of a suit, and again when he helps rescue Pip from Orlick; this marks a time in Pip's life when he realizes his real responsibilities and begins to act like a gentleman.

Wemmick

Wemmick illustrates one way of surviving in a society as hard and uncaring as the one he inhabits in London. His business and private lives are kept in watertight compartments and, as we get to know him better, we discover that there is much more to him than at first seems possible. The warm side of his nature which is so amply demonstrated in his relationships with his father, Miss Skiffins and Pip, has no place in the office he works in with Jaggers.

He helps Pip in many ways, noticeably with the attempt to save Magwitch, the setting up of Herbert in business, and in offering Pip hospitality in his home, which combines fantasy with the reality of true warmth and family love.

Mr Wopsle

Wopsle embodies the idea of aspirations, but they are aspirations that are as unreal in their attempted attainment as are Pip's ideas of what constitutes a gentleman. Wopsle is in many ways a caricature of Pip. Note how his 'reviewing his success and developing his plans' is a parody of the way in which Pip sits down to review his finances and list his obligations.

What happens
in each chapter

Chapter 1 In a bleak churchyard set in the marshlands of the Thames estuary stands Pip, considering the graves of his family. A desperately hungry, manacled convict terrorizes him. Under threat of a horrible death at the hands of a mysterious young man (who is supposed to be with the convict) Pip promises to return next morning with a file and food.

Chapter 2 At the village forge, Pip's home, Joe Gargery tells him that Mrs Joe is on 'the rampage' with 'Tickler', the punishment cane. Mrs Joe, Pip's elder sister by twenty years, lacks the maternal instinct, but Pip's hard life is tempered by his gentle, soft-hearted brother-in-law Joe, the blacksmith. Pip conceals his bread in order to take it to the convict but is dosed with tar water for bolting his food. Guns are heard during the evening; these signal a prisoner has escaped from the prison ships. Pip rises at dawn and steals more food and a file in order to placate his convict who is hiding out in the marsh.

Chapter 3 Pip approaches a figure in the misty marsh, but he discovers this is a different man, who has a scar on his face. Pip meets 'his' convict and when he informs him of another in the area he becomes agitated and files furiously at his leg irons as Pip slips away, hardly noticed.

Chapter 4 Christmas Day is a miserable occasion for Pip. Dressed in uncomfortable, formal clothes, oppressed by the insensitive, pretentious guests, especially Mr Pumblechook – a well-to-do relative of Joe's – Pip suffers agonies of guilt, fearing exposure as a thief. Dinner is interrupted by soldiers; a search party has arrived at the forge at the very moment Mrs Joe discovers that her pork pie is no longer in the pantry.

Chapter 5 Joe mends the handcuffs which are to be used when the escaped convict is located. Joe takes Pip to follow the hunt and they both watch the two convicts fighting like animals in the marsh mud. Before he is led back to the prison ship, Pip's convict confesses that it was he who stole the food and drink from the forge.

Chapter 6 Pip decides he will not confide in Joe about his part in the theft of the food because he is afraid Joe will not love him anymore. Mr Pumblechook and Mr Wopsle debate how the convict entered the house.

Chapter 7 It is a year later. Pip wants an education and with the help of Biddy he learns the basics at an evening school. Joe tells of his lack of schooling, his unhappy young life and his reasons for tolerating Mrs Joe's ill humour. Mrs Joe and Mr Pumblechook return from market full of excitement. They tell Pip he is to visit the grand home of the rich eccentric, Miss Havisham, to 'play'. They feel this is a great opportunity for the boy and that Miss Havisham might be instrumental in making Pip's fortune.

Chapter 8 Pip is met at the gate of Satis House by a beautiful but arrogant young girl – Estella. He is led through the darkened house to meet Miss Havisham. She sits surrounded by decay and decomposition, dressed in an ancient wedding dress which she has worn since she was deserted on her wedding day, long ago. Since that day she has lived a secluded, timeless existence and has only summoned Pip because she has a fancy to watch a child play. Estella is disdainful of Pip's common language and working-class clothing and manner. For the first time Pip is deeply hurt and ashamed of his lowly position. Before he leaves he wanders into the derelict brewery where he 'sees' a figure hanging from a beam; the image is that of Miss Havisham.

Chapter 9   On his return to the forge Pip is cross-questioned by Mrs Joe and Pumblechook and he invents stories of a coach, swords, flags and other fantastic happenings in order to satisfy them. Later he admits to Joe that he was lying and also that he is aware of being 'common'. Joe is shocked and warns Pip against dishonesty. Pip is too deeply affected by Estella to be able to shake off his new-found feelings of inferiority.

Chapter 10   Pip asks Biddy to teach him everything she knows; he hopes to become less common by achieving some kind of education. Later he goes to the inn, the Three Jolly Bargemen, to meet Joe. Here he finds Joe and Mr Wopsle in a stranger's company. This man questions Pip and stirs his drink with a file – the file Pip gave to the convict. As he leaves, the stranger gives Pip a shilling wrapped in a crumpled paper which is later found to be two pound notes.

Chapter 11   Pip makes a second visit to Miss Havisham. This time there are visitors in Satis House, poor relations who 'toady' to Miss Havisham in hopes of benefiting in her will. Pip walks Miss Havisham around a room where there is a huge table still laid with the rotted wedding breakfast. Miss Havisham expects to be laid out on this table when she is dead. The relatives are sent away disappointed. Pip and Estella play cards for Miss Havisham's entertainment but she gains more pleasure from encouraging Pip to admire Estella's beauty. Estella is again contemptuous of Pip. As Pip wanders in the gardens he meets a 'pale young gentleman' who challenges him to, and loses with good humour, a friendly boxing match. As he leaves, Estella allows Pip to kiss her cheek.

Chapter 12   Pip's visits to Miss Havisham continue. He regularly wheels her round the darkened rooms and plays cards with Estella while Miss Havisham mutters maliciously about breaking his heart. Joe is sent for and ordered to bring with him the indentures for Pip to be apprenticed to Joe as a blacksmith. This causes Mrs Joe and Pumblechook to speculate on Pip's future.

Chapter 13   Joe is totally confused in Miss Havisham's presence and directs all his conversation through Pip. This embarrasses Pip. Miss Havisham gives Joe twenty-five guineas as Pip's premium and tells them to expect no more from her. Later Mrs Joe and Pumblechook view this as good fortune and there is a celebration dinner at the Blue Boar. Pip does not find the evening enjoyable and makes himself miserable by contemplating the 'common' nature of a blacksmith's work.

Chapter 14   Pip recalls how he once looked forward to working alongside Joe at the forge. Now he is obsessed with a feeling of shame about his humble position and the way Estella would scorn him if she were to see him at work. Pip does not talk to Joe about his feelings.

Chapter 15   Pip continues to try to educate himself but his efforts to help Joe to learn end in failure. Joe agrees, with some reservation, to Pip taking a half-day holiday in order to visit Miss Havisham. Orlick – Joe's journeyman – resents this favouritism. He insults Mrs Joe and Joe is obliged to knock him down.

Pip's visit to Miss Havisham leaves him feeling even more discontented than before. Estella is abroad receiving a lady's education and Miss Havisham taunts Pip with the news that Estella is admired greatly by everyone.

Wopsle gives a recital at Pumblechook's home and when Pip finally returns to the forge he finds Mrs Joe has been attacked and has head injuries from which she will never recover.

Chapter 16   Pip's suspicions are aroused when a convict's leg iron is found near Mrs Joe. The cut is an old one and Pip feels it belonged to his old convict from years before. The police cannot solve the mystery but Pip suspects Orlick or even the stranger with the file at the Three Jolly Bargemen. Biddy joins the household to care for them all, especially Mrs Joe, now paralysed and unable to speak.

Chapter 17   Pip's apprenticeship continues and he makes yearly visits to Miss Havisham. Biddy becomes significant in Pip's life and he confides in her, telling her of Estella and the reason for his wish to become a gentleman. Biddy suggests he should not see life through Estella's eyes and that she is not worthy of his love. Pip says he would do better to fall in love with Biddy but she realistically states that he never will.

Biddy is concerned that Orlick is attracted to her; Pip feels Joe should dismiss him. Pip's resolve to face the future realistically is destroyed by the hope that Miss Havisham will one day make his fortune.

Chapter 18   Pip is in the fourth year of his apprenticeship. A stranger, Jaggers, who is a lawyer from London, arrives at the Three Jolly Bargemen. He is rather overbearing and humiliates Wopsle. He informs Pip that Pip has 'great expectations' but is not, at this stage, to know who his benefactor is. Pip assumes it to be Miss Havisham. He is to leave for London to be educated as a gentleman, but there is a feeling of loneliness in Pip as he goes to bed that night.

Chapter 19   Joe burns Pip's indentures and Pip takes a last walk through the familiar places of his childhood. He daydreams that in the future he will be able to behave with condescending generosity towards the villagers. Pip talks to Biddy about Joe, asking her to improve Joe so that he might later fit in with a better station in life. Biddy reminds Pip of Joe's pride and worth. Trabb and Pumblechook demonstrate the powerful effect of money upon their behaviour towards Pip. Pip visits Miss Havisham before leaving for London. She has heard from Jaggers of his expectations.

Chapter 20   Pip arrives in London and goes to Jaggers' office. This, and the area in which it is situated, has a sordid, even macabre, air. He observes Jaggers' professional handling of his clients and learns from him about his own financial arrangements. Pip then goes to Barnard's Inn where he is to lodge temporarily with Herbert Pocket.

Chapter 21   Wemmick takes Pip to Barnard's Inn, which is shabby and uninviting. Herbert is out but on his return welcomes Pip warmly. They recognize each other as the youthful boxers in the garden of Satis House.

Chapter 22   Herbert and Pip have dinner. Herbert demonstrates tact in helping to correct Pip's table manners. He gives him a nickname – Handel.

Pip learns the story of Miss Havisham. She was, in her youth, an heiress who was left a larger share of money than that of her half-brother. She fell in love with a man who persuaded her to part with a large sum of money. On her wedding day Miss Havisham found that she had been a victim of a confidence trick wrought by this man in conspiracy with her half-brother. From that moment Miss Havisham became an eccentric recluse.

Herbert is working in a counting house and has no 'expectations' from Miss Havisham. He takes Pip home to meet his father, Matthew, who is to be Pip's tutor.

Chapter 23   Pip meets his fellow students, Drummle and Startop, at the Pockets' home. He also learns about the Pocket family. Matthew, though a fine scholar, is hopelessly inadequate in practical matters. His wife is no better; born of an aristocratic family she is ineffectual in handling the organization of the family's domestic life.

Pip rows on the river with the other young men and decides to get a boat of his own.

Chapter 24   Matthew Pocket is Pip's tutor, and plans his education to fit his future life as a gentleman of leisure. Pip decides to continue to live with Herbert and consults Jaggers about his allowance. Wemmick, Jaggers' head clerk, takes Pip to see his formidable employer in action in court. He also shows him gifts from condemned criminals which he terms 'portable property', invites him to his Walworth home, and tells him to observe Jaggers' housekeeper when he dines at Jaggers' home.

Chapter 25   Pip studies in the Pockets' home. There, his dislike of Drummle grows. He is also faced with the 'toadying' Pockets who fawn upon him in his new-found wealth. His education develops alongside expensive habits. A visit to Wemmick's castle at

Walworth takes place. Here Pip sees the other side of Wemmick in this eccentric but loving home and meets the Aged Parent.

Chapter 26   Jaggers invites Pip and his fellow students to dine. Drummle, having drunk wine, boasts of his rowing prowess and generally behaves badly. Jaggers takes a great interest in him. Jaggers forces his housekeeper to show her strong wrists. Drummle's behaviour deteriorates. A month later he leaves the Pockets' household.

Chapter 27   A letter comes from Biddy saying Joe will visit Pip in London. Pip, snobbishly conscious of Joe's manners, dreads the visit. Joe brings news that Estella has returned to England and wants to see Pip. Joe is awkward, even comical, yet he is dignified enough to leave when he realizes Pip's stiff behaviour indicates he is not welcome there. Pip runs after Joe, but it is too late: he has gone.

Chapter 28   While travelling to Satis House Pip hears a conversation between two convicts who are being transported by coach, under guard. One is the man who gave Pip the two pound notes, years before. At the Blue Boar Pip reads a newspaper article in which Pumblechook is presented as the founder of Pip's good fortune.

Chapter 29   Pip goes to Satis House believing that Miss Havisham intends him for Estella. Orlick is now porter at the gate. Estella, by this time a beautiful woman, warns Pip that she has no heart. But, despite everything, he loves her with a romantic passion. Miss Havisham urges him to love Estella utterly. Jaggers dines with them but discloses nothing. Pip's neglect of Joe is evident when he returns to the Blue Boar, rapturizing over Estella and failing to visit the forge.

Chapter 30   Pip speaks to Jaggers and brings about Orlick's dismissal. In the village Pip's enjoyment of his superiority is spoiled by the mockery of Trabb's boy.

Back in London Herbert and Pip confide in one another – Pip tells of his love for Estella and Herbert speaks of his love for Clara, the daughter of a retired ship's purser. They go to see Wopsle in a performance of *Hamlet*.

Chapter 31   Wopsle's play is farcical. Pip and Herbert visit Wopsle backstage and invite him home to dinner. That night Pip has nightmares which confuse his expectations, hopes and aspirations.

Chapter 32   A note from Estella announces her arrival in London and Pip, overjoyed, goes to meet her coach at Cheapside. Whilst waiting, he meets Wemmick and accompanies him to Newgate prison. The sordid prison contrasts with Pip's vision of Estella. He feels a 'nameless shadow' when he sees Estella and ponders on the taint of crime which seems to surround him.

Chapter 33   Pip travels to Richmond with Estella whose behaviour suggests she is obeying orders. She tells Pip that he is expected to accompany her on various social occasions. She speaks of her dislike of the 'toadying' Pockets and enquires about Newgate and Jaggers.

Chapter 34   Pip leads an idle, extravagant life. He and Herbert join a young men's club, 'The Finches of the Grove', of which Drummle is also a member. Pip and Herbert realize the need to sort out their finances. A formal letter from Trabb and Co tells Pip that Mrs Joe is dead.

Chapter 35   Pip is shocked by his sister's death although he did not feel love for her. He thinks about her attacker. The funeral is a mixture of farce and insensitivity.

Biddy announces her intention to leave the forge and also states that Orlick still bothers her. Pip is angry when Biddy doubts his promise to visit the forge regularly.

Chapter 36   Pip has his twenty-first birthday and Jaggers informs him that he has a yearly income of £500. He will not tell Pip any more about his benefactor. Pip wants to help Herbert and consults Wemmick who suggests that Pip goes to Walworth to discuss it there, as his official view must differ from his off-duty view.

Chapter 37   At Walworth, Wemmick discusses Pip's plan for Herbert sympathetically and arranges for Pip to buy Herbert a partnership in a firm of shipping brokers. These arrangements are to be secret. Pip meets Miss Skiffins.

Chapter 38   Pip regularly escorts Estella but is made jealous by other suitors. She warns Pip that she cannot feel love and Miss Havisham, too, is caught in this trap. There is a quarrel between the two women. Drummle tells Pip that he knows Estella, and Pip is concerned that she should encourage such a character. The chapter ends with a story of an ominous threat which symbolizes Pip's predicament.

Chapter 39   Pip is now twenty-three and still knows nothing about his expectations. His education is completed and he lives in rooms in Garden Court with Herbert, who is now progressing in business.

One stormy night Pip is visited by a stranger whom he realizes is Magwitch, the convict from his childhood. It is a great blow to Pip to learn that Magwitch, not Miss Havisham, is his benefactor. Magwitch had worked hard in Australia and amassed a fortune which he is using to create a gentleman out of Pip. His return to England is solely in order to see Pip, but it places him in grave danger as the death penalty is applied to any transported convict who returns.

Pip's emotions are in turmoil. He realizes Miss Havisham only used him for her diversion and never intended him for Estella. Moreover, he has neglected Joe through his growing snobbery which has, in reality, been paid for by a convict. Nonetheless, Pip feels he must give safe shelter to Magwitch.

Chapter 40   In the early morning Pip falls over someone crouched on the staircase. Magwitch is disguised as a farmer and using his assumed name, Provis. Pip moves him to lodgings in Essex Street. A visit to Jaggers verifies the benefactor's identity. Pip suffers alone for five days until Herbert's return. Magwitch swears Herbert to secrecy.

Chapter 41   Pip tells Herbert he is determined not to accept any more money from the convict. The two friends consider the effect of this on Magwitch and decide to get him out of England for his own safety. It is felt that Pip, too, should leave England.

Chapter 42   Magwitch reveals his story. As an abandoned child, surviving how he could but often jailed for stealing, he became a hardened criminal. He met a man called Compeyson who was outwardly a gentleman but in reality a heartless criminal. Compeyson's companion, Arthur, had once helped him in a swindle involving an heiress. Much later both Magwitch and Compeyson were put on trial for their crimes but Compeyson was given only a light sentence because of his gentlemanly veneer. Magwitch was given fourteen years and in revenge he tried to thwart Compeyson's escape. After this Magwitch was transported for life and so had heard no more of Compeyson. Magwitch makes reference to his wife during the telling of his story.

Herbert informs Pip that Compeyson was Miss Havisham's lover and Arthur her half-brother.

Chapter 43   Pip realizes that Magwitch might be in danger from Compeyson. He feels he must visit Estella and Miss Havisham before going abroad. At the Blue Boar Pip has an unpleasant encounter with Bentley Drummle, who is dining with Estella that night.

Chapter 44   At Satis House Pip confronts both Miss Havisham and Estella. Miss Havisham admits her deception and Pip tells her how worthy are Matthew and Herbert Pocket. He declares his love to Estella but she is unmoved and tells him she is to marry Drummle. When Pip arrives in London he is warned in a note written by Wemmick that he must not go to his rooms.

Chapter 45   Pip spends a bad night in Hummums Hotel and in the morning goes to Wemmick's home. Wemmick has heard that Compeyson is in London and Pip's apartment is being watched. Wemmick suggests a plan to move Magwitch to the riverside house of Clara Barley, Herbert's fiancée, until he can be put on board a ship.

Chapter 46   Pip meets Herbert's Clara at her house. Magwitch, softened in character, is given a room at the top of the house. He agrees to leave England. As this would be by boat, Pip and Herbert decide to row regularly on the river in order to avoid drawing attention to themselves at a later date when they are effecting Magwitch's escape.

Chapter 47   During the weeks of waiting for an appropriate moment to get Magwitch away, Pip rows regularly on the river. He no longer uses Magwitch's money and is falling seriously into debt. Pip learns that he is being followed by Compeyson so he informs Wemmick by letter.

Chapter 48   Pip is dining with Wemmick and Jaggers when he receives a note from Miss Havisham asking him to see her on business. Pip is suddenly aware of a resemblance between Jaggers' housekeeper, Molly, and Estella. Wemmick tells Molly's life story on the way home. Pip learns that Molly once had a daughter.

Chapter 49   Pip visits Miss Havisham and realizes her loneliness and feels pity for her. When he explains how he has set up Herbert in business and why he can no longer do so, Miss Havisham arranges to pay the outstanding monies herself. Estella is now married to Drummle. Miss Havisham, though now filled with remorse, cannot tell Pip of Estella's parentage as she knows nothing of her before Jaggers brought the child to her. As Pip leaves, his old vision of Miss Havisham hanging in the brewery returns to his mind and this causes him to turn back. Miss Havisham's dress catches fire and, though Pip saves her, she is badly burned and shocked. Estella and the Pockets are to be informed. Miss Havisham is placed on the great table. Delirious, she murmurs about forgiveness and remorse.

Chapter 50   Herbert tells Pip all he has learned from Magwitch. Magwitch once had a wife and child. The woman murdered her rival in a jealous scene and as she had threatened to kill their child too, Magwitch believes that this has been done. Pip is convinced that Estella is Magwitch's daughter.

Chapter 51   Pip confronts Jaggers with his belief about Estella's parents but Jaggers avoids discussing this. After an appeal, with Wemmick's help, Pip extracts the full story. When Molly's case came to court Jaggers took her young child to Miss Havisham where she would be saved from a miserable existence. He took Molly as his servant. Pip is warned never to tell Estella as this knowledge would degrade her. Both Wemmick and Jaggers seem uncomfortable after showing humane feelings in each other's presence.

Chapter 52   Herbert is soon to go to the East to a new branch of Clarriker's. Wemmick eventually sends word that the time is right to move Magwitch. Pip and Herbert plan to take him down river in the rowing boat and put him aboard the Hamburg steamer. Pip then receives an anonymous note telling him to go to the marshes where he will learn something about 'Provis' (Magwitch). He visits Satis House, then dines at the Blue Boar, where he hears of Pumblechook's complaints. He finds he has lost the anonymous note.

Chapter 53   Orlick awaits Pip in the old sluice-house and tries to kill him. Herbert (who found the note), aided by Trabb's boy, saves him. Pip returns to London and in a day is well enough to continue with the plan for Magwitch's escape.

Chapter 54   The escape party rows down river and spends the night at a riverside inn. There is news of a mysterious boat in the vicinity. Pip sees two strangers looking at his boat. The next morning the escape plan fails when a police boat arrests them. Compeyson is a muffled figure aboard the police vessel. The steamer runs down Pip's boat and the two old enemies fight in the water. Compeyson is drowned but the badly wounded Magwitch, and his money, are taken by the police. Pip accompanies him.

Chapter 55   Magwitch's trial is to be in a month's time. Jaggers states there is no chance of acquittal or recovering his money. Pip is offered work with Herbert, but he delays his answer. Herbert leaves to take up his work in the East where Clara will later join him. Wemmick explains that he was deliberately misinformed about Compeyson's whereabouts on the day of the escape. Wemmick marries Miss Skiffins in a humorously secretive ceremony. He does not want Jaggers to be informed.

Chapter 56   Magwitch's condition worsens. He lies uncomplaining in the prison infirmary. Pip's daily visits create a loving bond between them. Magwitch is condemned to death, in company with thirty other criminals, but he dies before the day of execution. Pip's formal appeals for mercy are fruitless but Magwitch dies peacefully when Pip tells him that his daughter is alive, is a beautiful lady, and is loved by Pip.

Chapter 57   Pip, in considerable debt, falls ill in a delirious fever. Because of his condition he is not sent to a debtors' prison. When the delirium clears some weeks later, Pip recognizes his nurse as Joe. Joe, now able to write, sends word to Biddy of Pip's recovery. He tells Pip that Miss Havisham has died leaving Matthew Pocket £4000 in her will and only insulting amounts to the 'toadies'. There is news of Orlick, too; he has been put in prison for burgling Pumblechook's shop. Joe is tactful and gentle but as Pip's recovery advances he becomes increasingly respectful. Finally he settles Pip's debts and leaves without a word. Pip decides to go to the forge to ask Joe to forgive him and Biddy to marry him.

Chapter 58   Satis House is to be sold and pulled down. At the Blue Boar Pumblechook is no longer subservient to Pip. In the village Biddy's school is closed, and on arrival at the forge Pip is amazed to find that it is Biddy's and Joe's wedding day. Pip asks them to forgive him and his behaviour in the past, and they say emotional farewells.

Pip joins Herbert and Clara in the East. He works for Clarriker's as a clerk. He lives happily, writes regularly to Joe and Biddy and, over the years, pays off his debts. The secret of the origins of Herbert's partnership comes out. Herbert and Pip prosper, through their own efforts and efficiency.

Chapter 59   After eleven years in the East Pip returns to the forge. Joe and Biddy have a young son, named Pip, who reminds Pip of himself when young. Pip makes a sentimental visit to the grounds of Satis House. There he meets Estella, now widowed after years of unhappy marriage. She is changed by her years of suffering and asks Pip's forgiveness. Pip does not allow them to part, but takes her by the hand and, as the moon rises and dispels the mist, they leave the ruined garden together.

Coursework and preparing for the examination

If you wish to gain a certificate in English literature then there is no substitute for studying the text/s on which you are to be examined. If you cannot be bothered to do that, then neither this guide nor any other will be of use to you.

Here we give advice on studying the text, writing a good essay, producing coursework, and sitting the examination. However, if you meet problems you should ask your teacher for help.

Studying the text

No, not just read – study. You must read your text at least twice. Do not dismiss it if you find a first reading difficult or uninteresting. Approach the text with an open mind and you will often find a second reading more enjoyable. When you become a more experienced reader enjoyment usually follows from a close study of the text, when you begin to appreciate both what the author is saying and the skill with which it is said.

Having read the text, you must now study it. We restrict our remarks here to novels and plays, though much of what is said can also be applied to poetry.

1 You will know in full detail all the major incidents in your text, **why**, **where** and **when** they happen, **who** is involved, **what** leads up to them and what follows.

2 You must show that you have an **understanding of the story**, the **characters**, and the **main ideas** which the author is exploring.

3 In a play you must know what happens in each act, and more specifically the organization of the scene structure – how one follows from and builds upon another. Dialogue in both plays and novels is crucial. You must have a detailed knowledge of the major dialogues and soliloquies and the part they play in the development of plot, and the development and drawing of character.

4 When you write about a novel you will not normally be expected to quote or to refer to specific lines but references to incidents and characters must be given, and they must be accurate and specific.

5 In writing about a play you will be expected both to paraphrase dialogue and quote specific lines, always provided, of course, that they are actually contributing something to your essay!

To gain full marks in coursework and/or in an examination you will also be expected to show your own reaction to, and appreciation of, the text studied. The teacher or examiner always welcomes those essays which demonstrate the student's own thoughtful response to the text. Indeed, questions often specify such a requirement, so do participate in those classroom discussions, the debates, class dramatizations of all or selected parts of your text, and the many other activities which enable a class to share and grow in their understanding and feeling for literature.

Making notes

A half-hearted reading of your text, or watching the 'film of the book' will not give you the necessary knowledge to meet the above demands.

As you study the text jot down sequences of events; quotations of note; which events precede and follow the part you are studying; the characters involved; what the part being studied contributes to the plot and your understanding of character and ideas.

Write single words, phrases and short sentences which can be quickly reviewed and which will help you to gain a clear picture of the incident being studied. Make your notes neat and orderly, with headings to indicate chapter, scene, page, incident, character, etc, so that you can quickly find the relevant notes or part of the text when revising.

Writing the essay

Good essays are like good books, in miniature; they are thought about, planned, logically structured, paragraphed, have a clearly defined pattern and development of thought, and are presented clearly – and with neat writing! All of this will be to no avail if the tools you use, i.e. words, and the skill with which you put them together to form your sentences and paragraphs are severely limited.

How good is your general and literary vocabulary? Do you understand and can you make appropriate use of such terms as 'soliloquy', 'character', 'plot', 'mood', 'dramatically effective', 'comedy', 'allusion', 'humour', 'imagery', 'irony', 'paradox', 'anti-climax', 'tragedy'? These are all words which examiners have commented on as being misunderstood by students.

Do you understand 'metaphor', 'simile', 'alliteration'? Can you say what their effect is on you, the reader, and how they enable the author to express himself more effectively than by the use of a different literary device? If you cannot, you are employing your time ineffectively by using them.

You are writing an English literature essay and your writing should be literate and appropriate. Slang, colloquialisms and careless use of words are not tolerated in such essays.

Essays for coursework

The exact number of essays you will have to produce and their length will vary; it depends upon the requirements of the examination board whose course you are following, and whether you will be judged solely on coursework or on a mixture of coursework and examination.

As a guide, however your course is structured, you will be required to provide a folder containing at least ten essays, and from that folder approximately five will be selected for moderation purposes. Of those essays, one will normally have been done in class-time under conditions similar to those of an examination. The essays must cover the complete range of course requirements and be the unaided work of the student. One board specifies that these pieces of continuous writing should be a minimum of 400 words long, and another, a minimum of 500 words long. Ensure that you know what is required for your course, and do not aim for the minimum amount – write a full essay then prune it down if necessary.

Do take care over the presentation of your final folder of coursework. There are many devices on the market which will enable you to bind your work neatly, and in such a way that you can easily insert new pieces. Include a 'Contents' page and a front and back cover to keep your work clean. Ring binders are unsuitable items to hand in for **final** assessment purposes as they are much too bulky.

What sort of coursework essays will you be set? All boards lay down criteria similar to the following for the range of student response to literature that the coursework must cover.

Work must demonstrate that the student:

1 shows an understanding not only of surface meaning but also of a deeper awareness of themes and attitudes;

2 recognizes and appreciates ways in which authors use language;

3 recognizes and appreciates ways in which writers achieve their effects, particularly in how the work is structured and in its characterization;

4 can write imaginatively in exploring and developing ideas so as to communicate a sensitive and informed personal response to what is read.

Much of what is said in the section **'Writing essays in an examination'** (below) is relevant here, but for coursework essays you have the advantage of plenty of time to prepare your work – so take advantage of it.

There is no substitute for arguing, discussing and talking about a question on a particular text or theme. Your teacher should give you plenty of opportunity for this in the classroom. Listening to what others say about a subject often opens up for you new ways to look at and respond to it. The same can be said for reading about a topic. Be careful not to copy down slavishly what others say and write. Jot down notes then go away and think about what you have heard, read and written. Make more notes of your own and then start to clarify your own thoughts, feelings and emotions on the subject about which you are writing. Most students make the mistake of doing their coursework essays in a rush – you have time so use it.

Take a great deal of care in planning your work. From all your notes, write a rough draft and then start the task of really perfecting it.

1 Look at your arrangement of paragraphs, is there a logical development of thought or argument? Do the paragraphs need rearranging in order? Does the first or last sentence of any paragraph need redrafting in order to provide a sensible link with the preceding or next paragraph?

2 Look at the pattern of sentences within each paragraph. Are your thoughts and ideas clearly developed and expressed? Have you used any quotations, paraphrases, or references to incidents to support your opinions and ideas? Are those references relevant and apt, or just 'padding'?

3 Look at the words you have used. Try to avoid repeating words in close proximity one to another. Are the words you have used to comment on the text being studied the most appropriate and effective, or just the first ones you thought of?

4 Check your spelling and punctuation.

5 Now write a final draft, the quality of which should reflect the above considerations.

Writing essays in an examination
Read the question. Identify the key words and phrases. Write them down, and as they are dealt with in your essay plan, tick them off.

Plan your essay. Spend about five minutes jotting down ideas; organize your thoughts and ideas into a logical and developing order – a structure is essential to the production of a good essay. Remember, brief, essential notes only!

Write your essay
How long should it be? There is no magic length. What you must do is answer the question set, fully and sensitively in the time allowed. You will probably have about forty minutes to answer an essay question, and within that time you should produce an essay between roughly 350 and 500 words in length. Very short answers will not do justice to the question, very long answers will probably contain much irrelevant information and waste time that should be spent on the next answer.

How much quotation? Use only that which is apt and contributes to the clarity and quality of your answer. No examiner will be impressed by 'padding'.

What will the examiners be looking for in an essay?
1 An answer to the question set, and not a prepared answer to another, albeit slightly similar question done in class.

2 A well-planned, logically structured and paragraphed essay with a beginning, middle and end.

3 Accurate references to plot, character, theme, as required by the question.

4 Appropriate, brief, and if needed, frequent quotation and references to support and demonstrate the comments that you are making in your essay.

5 Evidence that reading the text has prompted in you a personal response to it, as well as some judgment and appreciation of its literary merit.

How do you prepare to do this?
1 During your course you should write between three to five essays on each text.

2 Make good use of class discussion etc, as mentioned in a previous paragraph on page 73.

3 Try to see a live performance of a play. It may help to see a film of a play or book, though be aware that directors sometimes leave out episodes, change their order, or worse, add episodes that are not in the original – so be very careful. In the end, there is no substitute for **reading and studying** the text!

Try the following exercises without referring to any notes or text.

1 Pick a character from your text.

2 Make a list of his/her qualities – both positive and negative ones, or aspects that you cannot quite define. Jot down single words to describe each quality. If you do not know the word you want, use a thesaurus, but use it in conjunction with a dictionary and make sure you are fully aware of the meaning of each word you use.

3 Write a short sentence which identifies one or more places in the text where you think each quality is demonstrated.

4 Jot down any brief quotation, paraphrase of conversation or outline of an incident which shows that quality.

5 Organize the list. Identify groupings which contrast the positive and negative aspects of character.

6 Write a description of that character which makes full use of the material you have just prepared.

7 What do you think of the character you have just described? How has he/she reacted to and coped with the pressures of the other characters, incidents, and the setting of the story? Has he/she changed in any way? In no more than 100 words, including 'evidence' taken from the text, write a balanced assessment of the character, and draw some conclusions.

You should be able to do the above without notes, and without the text, unless you are to take an examination which allows the use of plain texts. In plain text examinations you are allowed to take in a copy of your text. It must be without notes, either your own or the publisher's. The intention is to enable you to consult a text in the examination so as to confirm memory of detail, thus enabling a candidate to quote and refer more accurately in order to illustrate his/her views that more effectively. Examiners will expect a high standard of accurate reference, quotation and comment in a plain text examination.

Sitting the examination

You will have typically between two and five essays to write and you will have roughly 40 minutes, on average, to write each essay.

On each book you have studied, you should have a choice of doing at least one out of two or three essay titles set.

1 **Before sitting the exam**, make sure you are completely clear in your mind that you know exactly how many questions you must answer, which sections of the paper you must tackle, and how many questions you may, or must, attempt on any one book or in any one section of the paper. If you are not sure, ask your teacher.

2 **Always read the instructions** given at the top of your examination paper. They are

there to help you. Take your time, and try to relax – panicking will not help.

3 **Be very clear about timing, and organizing your time.**

(a) Know how long the examination is.
(b) Know how many questions you must do.
(c) Divide (b) into (a) to work out how long you may spend on each question. (Bear in mind that some questions may attract more marks, and should therefore take proportionately more time.)
(d) Keep an eye on the time, and do not spend more than you have allowed for any one question.
(e) If you have spare time at the end you can come back to a question and do more work on it.
(f) Do not be afraid to jot down notes as an aid to memory, but do cross them out carefully after use – a single line will do!

4 **Do not rush the decision** as to which question you are going to answer on a particular text.

(a) Study each question carefully.
(b) Be absolutely sure what each one is asking for.
(c) Make your decision as to which you will answer.

5 **Having decided which question** you will attempt:

(a) jot down the key points of the actual question – use single words or short phrases;
(b) think about how you are going to arrange your answer. Five minutes here, with some notes jotted down will pay dividends later;
(c) write your essay, and keep an eye on the time!

6 **Adopt the same approach** for all questions. Do write answers for the maximum number of questions you are told to attempt. One left out will lose its proportion of the total marks. Remember also, you will never be awarded extra marks, over and above those already allocated, if you write an extra long essay on a particular question.

7 **Do not waste time** on the following;

(a) an extra question – you will get no marks for it.
(b) worrying about how much anyone else is writing, they can't help you!
(c) relaxing at the end with time to spare – you do not have any. Work up to the very moment the invigilator tells you to stop writing. Check and recheck your work, including spelling and punctuation. Every single mark you gain helps, and that last mark might tip the balance between success and failure – the line has to be drawn somewhere.

8 **Help the examiner.**

(a) Do not use red or green pen or pencil on your paper. Examiners usually annotate your script in red and green, and if you use the same colours it will cause unnecessary confusion.
(b) Leave some space between each answer or section of an answer. This could also help you if you remember something you wish to add to your answer when you are checking it.
(c) Number your answers as instructed. If it is question 3 you are doing, do not label it 'C'.
(d) Write neatly. It will help you to communicate effectively with the examiner who is trying to read your script.

Glossary of literary terms

Mere knowledge of the words in this list or other specialist words used when studying literature is not sufficient. You must know when to use a particular term, and be able to describe what it contributes to that part of the work which is being discussed.

For example, merely to label something as being a metaphor does not help an examiner or teacher to assess your response to the work being studied. You must go on to analyse what the literary device contributes to the work. Why did the author use a metaphor at all? Why not some other literary device? What extra sense of feeling or meaning does the metaphor convey to the reader? How effective is it in supporting the author's intention? What was the author's intention, as far as you can judge, in using that metaphor?

Whenever you use a particular literary term you must do so with a purpose and that purpose usually involves an explanation and expansion upon its use. Occasionally you will simply use a literary term 'in passing', as, for example, when you refer to the 'narrator' of a story as opposed to the 'author' – they are not always the same! So please be sure that you understand both the meaning and purpose of each literary term you employ.

This list includes only those words which we feel will assist in helping you to understand the major concepts in play and novel construction. It makes no attempt to be comprehensive. These are the concepts which examiners frequently comment upon as being inadequately grasped by many students. Your teacher will no doubt expand upon this list and introduce you to other literary devices and words within the context of the particular work/s you are studying – the most useful place to experience and explore them and their uses.

Plot

This is the plan or story of a play or novel. Just as a body has a skeleton to hold it together, so the plot forms the 'bare bones' of the work of literature in play or novel form. It is however, much more than this. It is arranged in time, so one of the things which encourages us to continue reading is to see what happens next. It deals with causality, that is how one event or incident causes another. It has a sequence, so that in general, we move from the beginning through to the end.

Structure

The arrangement and interrelationship of parts in a play or novel are obviously bound up with the plot. An examination of how the author has structured his work will lead us to consider the function of, say, the 43 letters which are such an important part of *Pride and Prejudice*. We would consider the arrangement of the time-sequence in *Wuthering Heights* with its 'flashbacks' and their association with the different narrators of the story. In a play we would look at the scene divisions and how different events are placed in a relationship so as to produce a particular effect; where soliloquies occur so as to inform the audience of a character's innermost emotions and feelings. Do be aware that great works of fiction are not just simply thrown together by their authors. We study a work in detail, admiring its parts and the intricacies of its structure. The reason for a work's greatness has to do with the genius of its author and the care of its construction. Ultimately, though, we do well to remember that it is the work as a whole that we have to judge, not just the parts which make up that whole.

Narrator   A narrator tells or relates a story. In *Wuthering Heights* various characters take on the task of narrating the events of the story: Cathy, Heathcliff, etc, as well as being, at other times, central characters taking their part in the story. Sometimes the author will be there, as it were, in person, relating and explaining events. The method adopted in telling the story relates very closely to style and structure.

Style   The manner in which something is expressed or performed, considered as separate from its intrinsic content or meaning. It might well be that a lyrical, almost poetical style will be used, for example concentrating on the beauties and contrasts of the natural world as a foil to the narration of the story and creating emotions in the reader which serve to heighten reactions to the events being played out on the page. It might be that the author uses a terse, almost staccato approach to the conveyance of his story. There is no simple route to grasping the variations of style which are to be found between different authors or indeed within one novel. The surest way to appreciate this difference is to read widely and thoughtfully and to analyse and appreciate the various strategies which an author uses to command our attention.

Character   A person represented in a play or story. However, the word also refers to the combination of traits and qualities distinguishing the individual nature of a person or thing. Thus, a characteristic is one such distinguishing quality: in *Pride and Prejudice*, the pride and prejudices of various characters are central to the novel, and these characteristics which are associated with Mr Darcy, Elizabeth, and Lady Catherine in that novel, enable us to begin assessing how a character is reacting to the surrounding events and people. Equally, the lack of a particular trait or characteristic can also tell us much about a character.

Character development   In *Pride and Prejudice*, the extent to which Darcy's pride, or Elizabeth's prejudice is altered, the recognition by those characters of such change, and the events of the novel which bring about the changes are central to any exploration of how a character develops, for better or worse.

Irony   This is normally taken to be the humorous or mildly sarcastic use of words to imply the opposite of what they say. It also refers to situations and events and thus you will come across references such as prophetic, tragic, and dramatic irony.

Dramatic irony   This occurs when the implications of a situation or speech are understood by the audience but not by all or some of the characters in the play or novel. We also class as ironic words spoken innocently but which a later event proves either to have been mistaken or to have prophesied that event. When we read in the play *Macbeth*:

> *Macbeth*
> Tonight we hold a solemn supper, sir,
> And I'll request your presence.

> *Banquo*
> Let your highness
> Command upon me, to the which my duties
> Are with a most indissoluble tie
> Forever knit.

we, as the audience, will shortly have revealed to us the irony of Macbeth's words. He does not expect Banquo to attend the supper as he plans to have Banquo murdered before the supper occurs. However, what Macbeth does not know is the prophetic irony of Banquo's response. His 'duties. . . a most indissoluble tie' will be fulfilled by his appearance at the supper as a ghost – something Macbeth certainly did not forsee or welcome, and which Banquo most certainly did not have in mind!

Tragedy   This is usually applied to a play in which the main character, usually a person of importance and outstanding personal qualities, falls to disaster through the combination of personal failing and circumstances with which he cannot deal. Such tragic happenings may also be central to a novel. In *The Mayor of Casterbridge*, flaws in Henchard's character are partly responsible for his downfall and eventual death.

In Shakespeare's plays, *Macbeth* and *Othello*, the tragic heroes from which the two plays take their names, are both highly respected and honoured men who have proven their outstanding personal qualities. Macbeth, driven on by his ambition and that of his very determined wife, kills his king. It leads to civil war in his country, to his own eventual downfall and death, and to his wife's suicide. Othello, driven to an insane jealousy by the cunning of his lieutenant, Iago, murders his own innocent wife and commits suicide.

Satire   Where topical issues, folly or evil are held up to scorn by means of ridicule and irony – the satire may be subtle or openly abusive.

In *Animal Farm*, George Orwell used the rebellion of the animals against their oppressive owner to satirize the excesses of the Russian revolution at the beginning of the 20th century. It would be a mistake, however, to see the satire as applicable only to that event. There is a much wider application of that satire to political and social happenings both before and since the Russian revolution and in all parts of the world.

Images   An image is a mental representation or picture. One that constantly recurs in *Macbeth* is clothing, sometimes through double meanings of words: 'he seems rapt withal', 'Why do you dress me in borrowed robes?', 'look how our partner's rapt', 'Like our strange garments, cleave not to their mould', 'Whiles I stood rapt in the wonder of it', 'which would be worn now in their newest gloss', 'Was the hope drunk Wherein you dressed yourself?', 'Lest our old robes sit easier than our new.', 'like a giant's robe upon a dwarfish thief'. All these images serve to highlight and comment upon aspects of Macbeth's behaviour and character. In Act 5, Macbeth the loyal soldier who was so honoured by his king at the start of the play, struggles to regain some small shred of his self-respect. Three times he calls to Seyton for his armour, and finally moves toward his destiny with the words 'Blow wind, come wrack, At least we'll die with harness on our back' – his own armour, not the borrowed robes of a king he murdered.

Do remember that knowing a list of images is not sufficient. You must be able to interpret them and comment upon the contribution they make to the story being told.

Theme   A unifying idea, image or motif, repeated or developed throughout a work.

In *Pride and Prejudice*, a major theme is marriage. During the course of the novel we are shown various views of and attitudes towards marriage. We actually witness the relationships of four different couples through their courtship, engagement and eventual marriage. Through those events and the examples presented to us in the novel of other already married couples, the author engages in a thorough exploration of the theme.

This list is necessarily short. There are whole books devoted to the explanation of literary terms. Some concepts, like style, need to be experienced and discussed in a group setting with plenty of examples in front of you. Others, such as dramatic irony, need keen observation from the student and a close knowledge of the text to appreciate their significance and existence. All such specialist terms are well worth knowing. But they should be used only if they enable you to more effectively express your knowledge and appreciation of the work being studied.

Titles in the series